Smart Guide™

to

Starting a Small Business

About Smart Guides™

Welcome to Smart Guides. Each Smart Guide is created as a written conversation with a learned friend; a skilled and knowledgeable author guides you through the basics of the subject, selecting the most important points and skipping over anything that's not essential. Along the way, you'll also find smart inside tips and strategies that distinguish this from other books on the topic.

Within each chapter you'll find a number of recurring features to help you find your way through the information and put it to work for you. Here are the user-friendly elements you'll encounter and what they mean:

The Keys

Each chapter opens by highlighting in overview style the most important concepts in the pages that follow.

Smart Money

Here's where you will learn opinions and recommendations from experts and professionals in the field.

Street Smarts

This feature presents smart ways in which people have dealt with related issues and shares their secrets for success.

Smart Sources

Each of these sidebars points the way to more and authoritative information on the topic, from organizations, corporations, publications, Web sites, and more.

Smart Definition

Terminology and key concepts essential to your mastering the subject matter are clearly explained in this feature.

F.Y.I.

Related facts, statistics, and quick points of interest are noted here.

What Matters, What Doesn't

Part of learning something new involves distinguishing the most relevant information from conventional wisdom or myth. This feature helps focus your attention on what really matters.

The Bottom Line

The conclusion to each chapter, here is where the lessons learned in each section are summarized so you can revisit the most essential information of the text.

One of the main objectives of the *Smart Guide to Starting a Small Business* is not only to better inform you how to become a small-business owner, but to provide sound, professional advice to ensure that you meet your business objectives.

Smart Guide™
to
Starting a Small Business

Lisa Rogak

CADER BOOKS

John Wiley & Sons, Inc.

New York • Chichester • Weinheim • Brisbane • Singapore • Toronto

ISBN 0-471-31885-X

Printed in the United States of America

10 9 8 7 6 5 4 3 2 1

Contents

Introduction

According to Paul Reynolds, a professor of entrepreneurship at Marquette University, seven million American adults are currently pursuing plans to start their own businesses.

You're in good company. Actually, your odds of success are greatly improved simply because you picked up this book. Many people are no doubt sincere about their entrepreneurial urges, but they only make an occasional half-hearted effort at starting a business, and never quite pull together all that is necessary to launch a successful new-business venture. Instead of developing a comprehensive plan that will bring them, one step at a time, to their objectives, they muddle along and become prime candidates for the get-rich-quick schemes advertised in the backs of magazines and on late-night TV. Then, when these too-good-to-be-true ventures inevitably fail, they either give up on ever running a business again or think that they lack whatever it takes to become a business owner.

What is unfortunate is that these aspiring entrepreneurs are really not different from a Bill Gates or anybody else who has built a successful business from the ground up. Instead, what they lacked is what you are currently holding in your hands, a guide that would help them reach their goals.

When it comes to business—or anything else in life—who you know is important, of course, but what's even more necessary to your success is *what* you know. Because you probably haven't operated your own full-fledged business previously, you'll need to get a good, basic understanding of what it's like through educating yourself. Of course, book learning will never take the place of tried-and-true experience, but until the day you start your business and hit the ground running, the information in the *Smart Guide to Starting a Small Business* will give you a great head start.

Here you'll learn how to choose the business that best fits your personality and skills, how to find money to fund your venture, and how to announce to the world that your business exists. You'll also learn about the universal tools that are necessary to start your venture and the high-tech tools that will help your business run smoothly. In fact, you'll receive a formal education in everything you'll need to plan, start, and then operate your business for the first year.

Starting a business is not an easy task; it's hard, dirty work that requires you to think on your feet and to make decisions—many of which you'll live with for a long time—often in the blink of an eye.

But it's also among the most satisfying projects that you can accomplish in your life. Imagine creating a vital, working company that provides a useful, needed product or service, where no such enterprise existed before.

If you are ready to start on a journey that will provide you with more excitement, and panic, than any roller coaster—and also offer lots of rewards—then what are you waiting for? Let's go!

Why You and Why Your Own Business?

- Before you start your own business, have a clear idea of why you want to be your own boss.

- As a small business owner, you'll need to call on skills you probably already possess, such as stamina, self-reliance, and a sense of humor.

- Starting your own business can involve a great deal of risk-taking, but can pay off in rewards both monetary and personal.

- Keep one eye on your budget at all times, but remember that a new business more often succeeds due to lots of hard work than to a big bank account.

- Keep up on communicating with your family and friends so they don't feel left out.

- Developing and maintaining a positive attitude about your business will go a long way toward keeping you on the road to success.

Unless you've been sleeping under a rock for the last ten years, you already know that the new American Dream is not to win the lottery or write a best-selling novel, but to run your own business. A steep decline in job security, an endless stream of corporate mergers and acquisitions, and the widespread acceptance and respect given to people who run their own companies have all helped to build this fast-growing trend. But most often, the reasons why American men and women are becoming entrepreneurs in record numbers today tend to be more personal: if you are like most aspiring business owners, you are probably tired of long commutes and dealing with incompetent bosses and coworkers, but primarily, you also have a great idea for a business, know you could make it fly, and want to control your own fate.

All this is why you've picked up the *Smart Guide to Starting a Small Business*, and with it, you're taking the first step to reaching your dream.

Do You Have What It Takes?

If you ask around, you'll find that most of your friends, family, and even office colleagues would like to run their own businesses. If you then ask them why they aren't currently self-employed, or why they haven't even begun to plan their venture, you'll probably uncover a litany of excuses, from a lack of time to a chronically overdrawn checking account to simply not knowing what to do first.

Often, these excuses are easier to tackle than aspiring entrepreneurs think. Indeed, they may realize this but lack the fortitude required to start a business, and are instead using one of these other reasons to mask the lack of self-confidence they have about their own abilities.

This probably won't be the first time you hear it—nor certainly the last—but starting, running, and then succeeding at your own business takes a lot of work; in fact, usually more work than money. It also requires that an entrepreneur be comfortable with keeping lots of balls in the air at once. This requirement can be nerve-wracking for people who have never run their own business, since, especially in a large corporate setting, employees tend to be held responsible for one kind of assignment or department, with strict orders never to stray from it.

In addition, as a business owner, you will be required to set goals for the company and then do everything possible to fulfill them within the specified time frame, budget, and available resources. Sounds easy, right? Not so fast. Especially if you're starting a service-oriented business where you're the chief cook and bottle-washer, and as CEO, you have to answer phones, write checks, and placate customers, all within a five-minute period.

Therefore, it's important that if your primary reason for wanting to start a business is to make a lot of money, you should realize that the steps you will have to take to get to that point—not to mention the time it will take—may require more than you want to invest.

Similarly, if your main reason for starting a business is because you hate your current job or boss, you'd better rethink your strategies. There will be times in your business when you will have to repeatedly work fourteen hours a day, or bite your tongue when dealing with a difficult client, and you may actually look back fondly on a previous job because a) you never worked more than an eight-hour day, or b) you could hand the disagreeable tasks off to a coworker. In most cases, when you first start your business, it's you and only you who will have to answer to clients. Later, as you add employees to help with the workload, clients still may prefer to work with the owner, and when you've underestimated the time it would take to finish a project but promised the customer you'd have it ready by nine the next morning, it's you who is on the line, not your boss. *You* are the boss.

In any case, as a business owner you're going to have to love your work enough to continue to work through difficult situations. If you start a business because you're unhappy with your current professional or personal life, there may be times you regret starting your own show; but if the work is enjoyable and stimulating, the topic is entertaining, and you love what you're doing, you'll be better equipped to deal with the occasional downside of being self-employed.

That's why taking the time to honestly evaluate your motivations for starting your own business and closely examining your personal strengths and weaknesses will not only help pinpoint the areas to watch out for, but this research may even help you to refine your business idea, as you'll do in chapter 3.

Get a notebook to jot down thoughts, ideas, and observations that occur to you as you read this book. You'll also use this notebook to write your answers to the questions in the quizzes that appear throughout the book. These exercises are designed to help you create a vision of your future business and your future entrepreneurial life—as well as to help you succeed in business beyond your wildest dreams.

Self-Assessment Quiz 1

1. How often do you reach your personal and career goals within the time you have specified for them? How do you react when you are late?

2. Describe an instance when you've had to do whatever it took in order to fulfill a promise. Would you be willing to go to similar lengths when running your business? Come up with a hypothetical situation in your business where you would *not* want to go out on a limb. How would you handle it instead?

3. At work would you rather concentrate on one project at a time, or do you thrive on keeping lots of balls in the air while searching for more?

4. How do you work best: with an impossible deadline looming or with more time than you think you need? How have you reacted in the past when forced to work out of sync with your natural style?

5. Do you work better if you are surrounded by people or if you're by yourself?

6. Do you truly believe deep down that you can succeed at anything to which you set your mind? If not, what is standing in your way and what do you need to do to fix it?

7. If you make a decision and it turns out to be

STREET SMARTS

Not only is it important to evaluate your personal strengths and weaknesses, but also those of the market you would like your business to serve.

When Ed Strom of El Dorado Hills, California, decided he wanted to run his own business after retiring from twenty years of military service, he knew several things: He wanted his business to be a success from the beginning, so he could maintain his previous lifestyle. He also wanted to have some support to get his business up and running, so he picked a franchise. And he wanted a business that would be in demand.

"I picked cleaning because it seems to be the expanding service industry of this decade," he says. "I live in a very affluent area, and I saw a great need for it here." He's been running his Workenders franchise ever since.

STREET SMARTS

Sometimes a person falls into a business and doesn't know that she's become an entrepreneur until well into her new career. Patricia Owens left the rat race in the mid-1970s in Connecticut to move to Vermont and live in a cabin.

After a year, she got restless and decided to look for a job. She instead found a flea market with booth space available for rent. "I came home, and saw this fabulous wardrobe from years of working in the corporate world," she said. So she cleaned out her closet and rented a booth. When her old clothes were snapped up, she bought more from thrift stores and yard sales.

Today, her booth has expanded into two funky shops in the area, and some people drive for hours to buy her clothes.

wrong, how well do you admit the error and accept responsibility? Do you fix it yourself or look for someone else to do the work?

8. How do you envision your personal life two, five, and ten years down the road regardless of whether you start your own business or not? Where will you be living, and in what style?

9. In terms of your energy level, are you a natural hare, working best in short spurts interspersed with brief rest periods, or are you a turtle, where slow and steady wins the race?

10. What is the primary reason you want to start your own business? Be as honest as you can.

Starting and running your own business requires wisdom, self-confidence, and the ability to plug away day after day, knowing that your sweat and long hours will result in a worthy goal: the satisfaction of succeeding at a business that would not have seen the light of day without your efforts. Being aware of your strengths and weaknesses in advance will go a long way toward developing the skills necessary to help you succeed.

The Skills You'll Need

In the past, many people believed that having an advanced degree in business was an absolute minimum requirement if you wanted to become an entrepreneur. Although the idea of running your own business may be a bit intimidating at first, happily, the outlook for business owners is different today. There is a great wealth of information available to help the budding entrepreneur—in books and seminars, through mentors, and from professionals such as accountants and lawyers. It's also possible to farm out the tasks and jobs you don't like to do, or for which you lack patience or skill, to trained professionals. Of course, you'll have to pay for the privilege, but when you compare the time and energy required to learn and then perform this work against the more productive and lucrative ways you could be spending that time, it makes sense to delegate out these tasks and pay the going rate.

Of course, in order to effectively communicate with these business people as well as with your own employees and colleagues, you'll need a familiarity with common business terms and concepts, which this book will provide. But first, here is a rundown of the basic skills you'll need in order to run your own show.

Stamina

Running a business can be one of the most stressful challenges you'll ever experience. The pressure and excitement can sap your energy and make it difficult to get up and go every day, even if you love what you do. Some people use an overabundance of alcohol, food, or sleep to deal with the stress, while others know that in order to maintain a healthy equilibrium during the particularly hairy times, they need to pay attention to their health.

Even when a million things are competing for your attention, it's a good idea to try to stay aware of the healthy things you can do to counteract the stress that results from being your own boss. Because, after all, you do want to be around to reap the rewards of all of your hard work.

Self-Discipline

When you were growing up, were you the kid who had to stay inside and practice the piano when the other kids on the block were outside playing ball?

Once you start your own business, you'll need to practice this kind of self-discipline in order to succeed. You should not feel guilty about wanting to devote yourself to your business, as long as you allow some time for leisure activities and strive for both a work life and a home life.

Some people use their business as a crutch to avoid dealing with unpleasant issues in their personal lives, or they become so addicted to the entrepreneurial rush that they neglect important moments in their lives, missing family gatherings, their children's events, or social or civic activities. These problems are symptomatic of an unhealthy work life and need to be addressed.

The pendulum may swing wildly between work and play, but you will start to sense the balance between home and work that feels right for you.

Self-Reliance

When it comes down to the wire and the hard decisions must be made, do you (a) hem and haw and wait for a miracle, or (b) take a deep breath, flip a coin, and prepare yourself to accept the consequences of your choice?

Nobody likes to be the one to make the difficult decisions. But if you're the one in charge, whether you have a hundred employees or just one, the buck will always stop with you. Being the one person who is ultimately responsible for the myriad successes and failures of your business means that you have to train yourself to take action when necessary, and not merely react. Fortunately, this is a trait that you can teach yourself. If you've been in a reactionary mode in your current work, be prepared to switch gears from the first day your feet hit the ground in your own business venture.

Flexibility

Nothing about running a business is predictable. People who tend to thrive as entrepreneurs are those who were bored as employees because they knew exactly what they would be doing when they got up in the morning.

There are chaos junkies, and then there are those who view life through a rigid viewfinder. Somewhere in that vast middle are entrepreneurs, who need to borrow a little from each side. After all, once you're running your business you need to be flexible enough to change your strategy when powers beyond your control flex their muscles, yet you need to stick to your guns when forces all around you are compelling you to change. Again, it's a question of balance, and you should expect to make mistakes while you try to find your own best middle ground. It's all a part of the entrepreneurial life.

SMART MONEY

Chuck Woodbury had very little money to spare when he started publishing his quarterly newspaper *Out West*, in which he writes about people and places in the western part of the country. He came up with the idea for the paper about halfway into a two-year stint traveling around the West in an RV.

He loved to travel and he loved to write: why not combine them? Today, *Out West* is a thriving quarterly publication, even with its low overhead, but Woodbury hasn't strayed from his early frugal days.

"It's important to keep your overhead really low," he says. "Don't get carried away with equipment, even though it's easy to become addicted to new technology."

Drive to Succeed

How badly do you need to win? What are you prepared to do in order to get there?

As an entrepreneur, you will at times be called on to break all the rules and do whatever it takes to grow your business. This could range from tapping out your personal financial reserves to hopping on a plane and flying all day to win over a new account.

Do you give up easily when a hard challenge looms? Or do you lick your lips with relish, knowing that you will be pushed to well beyond your limits in order to succeed at a given project or task? Though this may appear to be a skill that some people are born with, it's not. Frequently it's the people who are the most unenthusiastic about their responsibilities when working for someone else who break out with incredible energy and ideas when they start their own businesses.

A People Person

Whether it's coworkers, colleagues, or clients, and even if you spend most of your day working by yourself, you'll still need basic people skills to communicate with customers and to let them know about your business in the first place. If your business is the kind where you are surrounded by people all day long, you may tend to compensate for the overload by playing a hermit at night.

Try to keep in touch with your people limits so that you know when you need to take a break. Otherwise, you could lose a customer along with your temper when you start to approach the breaking point. Always keep in mind that you should treat every person you meet in the course of doing business with the same kind of attention and respect that you expect from other people.

A Sense of Humor

This is perhaps the most valuable skill you could ever have as a business owner. Sometimes life gets so absurd, and the challenges involved in running a company become so great that a time-out for laughter is necessary. Laughing at it all not only helps you regain your perspective, but it also provides several of the same physical benefits as does exercise. Peter McLaughlin, author of the book *CatchFire* says that "laughter stimulates many of the same positive physiological changes as exercise: deeper breathing, lower heart rate, decreased blood pressure, and a general feeling of relaxation. Humor engenders a powerful, even somewhat miraculous sense of balance, perspective, and joy that allows you to flourish in the midst of a tough business environment."

So go ahead and laugh: it's good for you—*and your business.*

Understanding the Risks ... and Rewards

Think back to a time in your life when you had to do without some aspect of the security that so many people today take for granted: comprehensive health insurance coverage, a reliable car that starts on the first try, a regular paycheck. How well were you able to deal with the situation? Did you shrug and think that if you had it before, you will have it again, or did you constantly obsess about the bad things that could happen as a result of going without?

Congratulations! You've just had a glimpse into the crystal ball of your future business. No matter what type of company you choose to run, or what kind of customer you'll pursue, or even whether you plan to work out of your home, an outside office, or a retail store, chaos will be the rule of your day, never the exception. And risk will become your mantra, because you will be making all the decisions and shouldering all the responsibility, when things go right and when they don't.

One business expert referred to running a business as legalized gambling, and he was right. Not only are you betting that you will succeed at business, but since being an entrepreneur spills over the borders into all areas of your life, you will in essence be gambling with your personal life. Right now, aren't you just a bit unsure about how the process of starting a business and doing what you need to do to make it thrive will affect your family, friends, and your own well-being?

It's possible to be aware of some of the risks connected with being an entrepreneur before you open your doors for the first time, but it's also important to admit what you *don't* know.

A Matter of Time

One of the biggest risks in running a business is that you will simply run out of time: time to complete a particular project, a time frame in which you have projected that your business would begin to show a profit, time to keep up with the often insurmountable paperwork. In the jam-packed days that most Americans put up with today, time is the most precious natural resource you have. And an entrepreneur who may have started a business against the advice of family and friends who think he's crazy for walking away from the security of a steady job is perennially aware of the ticking of the clock, especially if he's been given a deadline to succeed or shut the business down.

Frequently, a business owner is tempted to cut corners in order to fit everything in under the deadline. Some may accomplish this by cutting corners on quality or service, or by saying yes to every project that comes in the door, even though they wouldn't be able to get everything done if they worked twenty hours a day, seven days a week. If you feel yourself careening in this direction, the first thing you should do is to stop for a few minutes and take a deep breath. Try to clear your mind, and then focus on the context of the deadline as well as the overall picture of your business. Consider that this is only one—or even the first— of many deadlines you will have to meet over the course of a long, fruitful business career. Keeping your perspective is essential to running a growing and healthy business.

This next piece of advice is the single most important lesson you can learn, especially if your business requires you to adhere to strict deadlines: Train yourself to allow 10 to 20 percent more time to complete a project than you normally would budget. This goes against an entrepreneur's natural tendencies, where she's usually rushing around at breakneck speed all the time, trying to do ten things at once.

Where there are great risks you must take,

F.Y.I.

One of the best ways to create more time is to know when the worst times are for getting a particular task done. For instance, the worst time to catch someone on the phone tends to be Monday mornings from 9 A.M. to 11 A.M., which is when many people are rested up from the weekend and eager to dive right into their work. Of course, what frequently happens is that you end up playing telephone tag for the rest of the week if you're unable to reach a person on the first try.

SMART DEFINITION

Bootstrapping

A method of financing a business that is accomplished by having more creativity than dollars. The original term means having the stamina and inventiveness to pull yourself up by your bootstraps and keep going no matter what it takes.

there are also significant rewards. In time, the monetary reward that comes from being a successful entrepreneur can be sizable. But time and again, most successful business owners cite the psychic rewards as being far more satisfying than any financial rewards they have reaped.

In fact, once you become an entrepreneur one of these intangible rewards may come sooner than you imagined. Not long after your business starts to have some degree of visibility in your community and your industry, people will come looking to you for advice. Since you were able to succeed in business after such a short time—forget about the fact that you've just survived your most chaotic day as an entrepreneur yet—you are an expert in their eyes.

Show Me the Money!

The get-rich-quick mail-order business kits advertised in the back of magazines work hard to convince you that it's possible to rake in $2,000 a day while sitting at home in your bunny slippers, working only an hour or two each day. The truth is, in most cases, succeeding in business is due to lots of hard work, not the amount of money you're able to invest. If you have lots of cash to start your business, that's great; you'll avoid some of the more harrowing times that result when a client's check is late arriving and payroll is due. It will also mean you have more energy to devote to your business because you don't have to worry about where the money will come from.

And even though you may have some significant successes in the early days of running your

Your Baby

Why do you hear so many entrepreneurs refer to their businesses as their babies? Well, think about it: After all, you gave birth to it and raised it and actively influenced its direction and growth in its formative years. Don't parents do the same thing with their children? Once you get your business off the ground, you will never question why so many entrepreneurs refer to their companies as their babies.

One of the great perks of entrepreneurial success is when you glance back fondly at your chaotic early days and find that you've blocked out all the stress, strain, and lack of sleep that were necessary to propel you to the helm of a thriving company in the first place. Much like parenthood.

business—winning new clients or pulling in sales that are double your projected figures—it does not necessarily mean you're on the road to riches. On the contrary, because you're so determined to make your business succeed, you'll probably pour unexpected cash windfalls back into the company, whether it's to upgrade a computer system, hire a new employee, or invest in more advertising.

Frequently, finding the money to start a business is not the major problem that many people think it is; through a combination of creativity, negotiation, and some fancy footwork, banks, credit cards, and family can indeed come through for aspiring entrepreneurs. For more details on where to find the money and how to get it, see chapter 5, "Money, Money, Money."

Floating Your Bills

One of the main problems that people run into in their first year of business is surprisingly mundane: How will you pay the normal household bills and expenses when the business is playing Godzilla with your cash flow and you can't afford to pay yourself a salary? How are you going to keep a roof over your head?

Most financial experts advise that you start planning for your business far enough in advance to have a sizable financial cushion—enough to live on for a year—but let's face it: in the real world, such plans are not so feasible unless you come into a large inheritance or win the lottery.

The most common way to get a business off the ground and to keep the household bills paid is to have a supportive partner or spouse with a regular paycheck. Sometimes, this is negotiated by a series of trade-offs the couple makes together: If I can start my business and you pay the bills, when the business is pulling its own in a couple of years, then you can start your business, or go back to school, or take a year off.

To streamline your financial situation and thus reduce your monthly household obligations, it's a good idea to pay off as much credit card debt and other loans as you can. If you can't manage to pay all or most of it off, you should look into consolidating your total debt. (You may even want to trade in your current car for an older model to reduce your car payments.) Once you open your doors for business, you'll want to have as much cash as possible to sink into the business. You'll also want to have money available for emergencies and for paying your household bills on time.

Reducing your monthly debt obligations is one way to do it. You may also want to choose this time to refinance your mortgage in order to lower your monthly payments and free up more cash for the business.

With the advent of home-equity credit programs—paid out either as a loan or available as a line of credit you can tap into when necessary—many entrepreneurs are taking advantage of years of mortgage payments to draw on money to start their businesses. The interest rates are lower, but since such programs put your house at risk should your business's income slow down, you should consider this option carefully.

Whatever you choose, make sure to apply for these programs before you leave your current job while you can show as much household income as possible. Later, based on just one paycheck and the shakiness of a new enterprise, banks and credit companies may not look as favorably on your status.

Family and Friends

Do the people in your life think you have gone absolutely bonkers because you want to start your own business?

Good! Not only does it mean they're probably a little bit jealous of you, but it will also add some fuel to your fire and keep you plugging away at your business. Here's a little secret: Many of history's most famous entrepreneurs have kept their businesses going because their number one concern was to prove some naysayer wrong.

With that said, you should also understand that even though your family and friends may whole-

F.Y.I.

If you can't beat 'em, join 'em. That's exactly what many families do when one member starts a business that takes off rapidly. But according to a 1997 study by Arthur Andersen, today's family businesses are not mom and pop shops, but full-fledged companies that are thriving and growing concerns. Over 3,000 businesses were surveyed, and the median gross revenue of the reporting businesses was $10 million, with an average of fifty employees.

There are pros and cons to running a family business—like not being able to talk about anything else at family gatherings—but of people who have worked in both family-run companies and in enterprises run by outsiders, most prefer the clan operations.

heartedly support your efforts in the beginning, the stresses, long hours, and hard work required to start a business may make them—and you—second-guess and doubt your intentions and abilities later on.

Even though you may develop your business plan down to the tiniest detail, it's impossible to predict what your fledgling company will require of you. This unpredictability may make you a bit insecure at times, but be forewarned that it may turn your largest support group—your friends and family—against you when they think you do not have much time for them anymore.

In the best of all worlds your partner is also an entrepreneur, or has started a business in the past and is familiar with the ups and downs of running a business. Not only can he help you learn what to expect, but he is also apt to be more tolerant of your time commitments than a partner who has never started a business. This kind of understanding will undoubtedly become more common as more and more spouses become entrepreneurs.

In the meantime, the best thing to do is to sit down with your family, friends, and other people with whom you regularly spend time and spell out your expectations of how life will change for you—and them—once your business gets under way. Talk about your hopes and fears, and then ask them about their concerns. Develop plans together along with ways to handle the difficult situations that may come up. Try to plan a non-business family event once a week where everyone gets together and absolutely no business is discussed. Also make it clear that anyone can bring up new problems and concerns at any time, but that they all should also understand that starting and running a business is an all-consuming passion.

If you're working out of your home, you'll need to draw up specific times and areas in the house that are reserved for family use only, with others set aside for business purposes only. The best solution to this problem is to keep regular business hours and to have a separate office where you can close the door at the end of the day, and turn the ringer off the phone so you won't be tempted to answer it after hours. (You'll learn more about home offices in chapter 3.)

If you show your family that you're supportive of their needs while also being devoted to the business, a balance between work and leisure activities can be achieved.

Attitude Adjustment

Does your enthusiasm bubble quickly burst when someone makes a negative comment about a project on which you've worked? When you've been involved in an engrossing project that you loved but others couldn't understand why you spent so much time on, were you able to stay positive about it and continue working? Or did you start to lose interest, and eventually throw in the towel because you lacked their approval?

Attitude is everything when it comes to starting and successfully operating a business. A positive attitude surely will help you through the rough spots, but you shouldn't be naive. Taking things at face value may be the best way to interact with your family and friends, but when it comes to dealing with suppliers who promise you the moon and customers who demand it, you will need to be firm but reasonable. Believe what you are told, but since

WHAT MATTERS, WHAT DOESN'T

What Matters
• Outlook: The way you see your own abilities can be the sole predictor of the success of your business. Convince yourself that you can do anything to which you set your mind.

• Honesty to yourself and your family about your goals.

• Stubbornness. If you don't believe in your business, who will?

What Doesn't
• Perfectionism. It can bog down your business. So learn to let a few things slide.

• Money. It helps, but self-confidence and drive are probably more important assets in the long run.

• Stubbornness. Entrepreneurs can be among the most mule-headed individuals on the planet. Flexibility is a virtue, you just have to know when to use it.

the customers and suppliers you will deal with every day are probably dealing with their own chaotic lives—just like you—don't be surprised when a promise gets broken. Try to renegotiate, laugh about it, and continue to treat people with the respect they deserve.

Developing an attitude that contains the apparently contradictory combination of optimism and cynicism will go a long way in helping you take immediate action when necessary, and putting off the little things that can wait. When you're first starting out and bursting with enthusiasm, surprises you could never have predicted in a million years will come up. If you maintain a positive outlook—the optimism—yet keep on the alert and look for problems that may arise—the cynicism—you'll be better able to operate your business on an even keel.

Perhaps the most important aspect to maintaining a positive attitude is to make sure you spend at least one afternoon a week—or a full day if you can swing it—doing something that is not business related. Running a business requires the stamina of a marathoner; sprinters burn hot and fast and frequently end up extinguishing themselves very quickly. Marathoners have staying power. To be in it for the long haul you need to schedule downtime for yourself. Taking this time will give you the freshness to quickly react to business problems that require an immediate solution and the composure to keep your eyes on the big picture—your success as an entrepreneur.

What Comes Next?

Now that you've learned a little more about what it takes to run a business, and you have a clearer idea of where you'll excel and where you need a little help, you need to apply the same formula to the process of choosing your business. Because while anyone can start a business, the best way to run it into the ground is to start the *wrong* kind of business. You'll learn how to sort the chaff from the wheat in the next chapter.

THE BOTTOM LINE

So there's a little bit more to this business stuff than you had thought, right? Running a business is not like working at a job; many employees are able to leave the job behind when they leave the office. It's not that simple when you're running the show.

View this pre-business stage, when you're gathering your information and making your plans, as the calm before the storm. Relish the opportunity to take the time to project how you will benefit—and how your life will change—once your business is up and running. Remember, attitude is everything.

Choosing Your Business

When it comes to starting a business, many people are under the misconception that anyone is able to start any kind of business they want; all that's necessary is the drive to succeed.

Wrong, wrong, wrong. While entrepreneurial drive is vitally important to keeping a business going, if you're running a company that's the wrong fit for you or involves a topic in which you have absolutely no interest, you might as well not even open your doors in the first place. Even when you've narrowed it down to a particular field, it's still possible to refine it further to make the business fit your goals and temperament still more precisely. After all, if you're not in love with the idea of your business, you're starting out with not one but three strikes against you.

What Do You Want to Do?

You may think you already know what kind of business you want to run, what you plan to name it, and how much business you will be able to rake in during the course of your first year. Congratulations! You fall into a very small category of people who have their businesses planned down to the smallest detail, complete with a raft of contingency plans.

You're also in the minority. Many people first think of the type of business they'd like to run, and then spend months ironing out the details. And even when you think you have everything nailed down, once you open your doors for business, a whole new layer of details you hadn't anticipated will be there to greet you with open arms.

Regardless of which category you belong to, start by asking yourself the following questions:

• What do you really enjoy doing?

• If you could do anything, what would you like to do?

• If you're currently mulling over a particular idea for a business, is it really something you would look forward to doing on a daily basis, twelve or more hours a day?

• Have you picked this idea because it offers a popular product or service, and you think you'll be able to make more money with this business than with something you'd be happier doing? If you love working with people, then starting a service-oriented business where you have to deal with people all day makes sense. Starting a business where you have to be holed up in an office all day with no one around doesn't.

What Don't You Want to Do?

Think about the last job you had that you really hated. Didn't you start to resent getting out of bed every morning, knowing you were not going to enjoy yourself for at least the next eight hours of your day?

Now think about not only slaving away at that job but also assuming responsibility for every facet of it, from worrying about exceeding your budget to having to forego receiving your paycheck every so often because a customer decided to not pay a bill on time. *Now* how would you feel about your job?

Welcome to the life of an entrepreneur who selected the wrong business to start! Sure, you want to be your own boss, and reading stories about successful business owners who drive brand-new Mercedes and live in big expensive houses certainly makes running your own business sound appealing. But think about this: not only did famous entrepreneurs like Bill Gates and Ben and Jerry get to where they are today with plenty of hard work and long hours, *but they also loved what they were doing.* They *had* to, otherwise they wouldn't have invested so much of themselves into the company. They didn't start by paying a mail-order firm several hundred bucks for a kit to start a "can't miss" business they read about in an ad in the back of a magazine; they recognized a market that needed a product or service they could provide with their talents and hard work.

In order to succeed in your own business, you must take the same path that these entrepreneurial pioneers traveled. There's simply no other way. And there is nothing you could do professionally that will give you more enjoyment or satisfaction than starting and running your own business. So, now is the time to be painfully honest about your dreams, beliefs, and goals for your business and personal life, before you sink thousands of dollars and countless hours of work into a business that isn't right for you from the start.

Even if you already have a specific idea for a business in mind, answer the following questions in as much detail as possible to help you start to discover the best kind of business for you.

Self-Assessment Quiz 2

1. What are some favorite things you like to do in your spare time?

2. Name a time when you've seen another person making a living by working with one of your favorite hobbies. Could you adapt it in a similar fashion?

3. What were some of your favorite activities when you were a child? Name five different businesses that could result from these interests.

4. What subjects and activities did you excel at during your school years? What classes did you dread participating in?

5. What kind of person do you most enjoy spending time with? It's not necessary to name a specific person; instead, you should list a category, such as elderly women, kindergartner, young mothers, etc. Think of five businesses you would like to run that would cater to your favored group.

6. Go through the Help Wanted ads. What kind of jobs usually sound appealing to you?

7. If you could imagine yourself running any kind of business, what would it be? Then ask yourself what is preventing you from making this your business. What changes would you need to make in your life so this could work?

8. Perform a brainstorming exercise: In a stream-of-consciousness fashion, write down fifty things

F.Y.I.

If you think the term *location* pertains only to real estate, you're wrong. When you analyze the competition you will face, note how many have followed this philosophy. For those businesses that are weak on location, check out the ways in which they've compensated for being a bit out of the way.

Keep in mind that on the Internet, however, location is everything when it comes to the search engines. Registering your site so that it comes up in the first ten sites listed when a user punches in a term that could describe your business could mean the difference between building a web business that is not dependent upon your physical location, but on your *virtual* location.

you like to do at work and play. Be as brief as you can. When you're done, look at your list and see if any items can be combined into one business. Even try combining those that don't seem to make much sense; after all, there have been odder business combinations than a business that sells books, produces theatrical events, baby-sits neighborhood dogs, and serves three meals a day. Don't forget that unusualness helps.

After you have finished writing, consider the ideas that are particularly appealing to you. Then, think about the people you like to be with and all the things you most like to do. How can you combine these into one business?

Service or Product?

Basically, all businesses fall into one of two general categories: either they provide a *service* to a person or to another business, or they manufacture a *product*. There are infinite variations on each of these themes, but most businesses can be categorized in either of these ways.

It's important to realize that a service-oriented business doesn't necessarily mean that you need to be a people person, since landscapers and house-sitters—which are clearly both service businesses—spend very little face-to-face time with their clients. In the same light, a product-oriented entrepreneur who has decided to manufacture and sell her prize-winning salsa may spend most of her waking hours selling her product in person to supermarket managers and individual customers, not in the kitchen chopping and prepping vegetables.

Before you choose a specific business category,

How Much Do You Want to Succeed?

How badly do you think you want to succeed? Some people will go to great lengths to make sure that their business turns out the way they knew it would all along.

Back in 1988, Andrew Morrison was finishing up an engineering degree at Rennselaer Polytechnic Institute. He was also president of the student body and served on the school's board of trustees, where he regularly came in contact with the heads of Fortune 500 companies. "I looked at these guys, and thought they didn't look too much smarter than me." Despite his major, he preferred marketing, and upon graduation he founded his own marketing company, called Nia Direct.

The business was on shaky ground, however, and it almost went under. Morrison was determined to save it, and so he worked full-time as a computer programmer from four to midnight and devoted his days to his business. After a couple of years at this breakneck pace, his company was starting to thrive so he quit his night job to devote himself to Nia Direct. Today he develops marketing campaigns for AT&T and Lever Brothers.

try to get a strong feel for the way you will spend the majority of your time. Remembering, of course, that you can always delegate tasks that don't play to your strongest skills. And once you have a good idea of the type of business that will make you happiest, start to do your homework. Subscribe to the trade magazines in your chosen field and talk to people who are already running that kind of business. Some aspiring entrepreneurs even spend their vacations interning for the types of businesses they're leaning toward. Immersing oneself in the lifestyle for a week or two is a great way to determine if the business will be a great fit or not.

For instance, many people who stay at an inn or bed and breakfast look misty-eyed at the innkeepers and dream aloud of trading places. Most inn-

F.Y.I.

Typically, a service-oriented business is the most prevalent type among new entrepreneurs for several reasons: it's easy to start, since many are run as sole proprietorships (a form of business in which you as owner are personally liable for the entire business); it usually requires a small investment; and it doesn't matter if you run the business from your home, though you may go out to visit your customers.

Assess your skills with an impartial eye, and practice on willing friends to get a feel for what it would be like to provide your talent to people who will in turn pay you for your services. Once you do, you may never look at your hobbies in quite the same way.

keepers would probably take them up on it, since it would mean an end to scrubbing toilets and being wide awake and cheerful when greeting latecomer guests at 11 P.M.—after getting up at five that morning to cook breakfast. The grass is always greener on the other side until you get to walk on it yourself. Then, the hidden thorns and burrs may cause you to have second thoughts.

To further whittle down your business choices, write down the answers to the following questions in your notebook.

Self-Assessment Quiz 3

1. In your own words, how do you define a service-oriented business? Who would you rather be in service to: individual consumers, businesses, or nonhumans—like houses, plants, or dogs, cats, and other animals?

2. Would you rather work out of one office, or live a more freelance type of life, working from your home or moving to a new workplace each time a work project changes?

3. Do you want to run a business where you'll be doing work that is similar to the kind of job you're doing presently, or do you want to do something totally different and make a complete career change? Or does your ideal business fall somewhere in the middle of the two?

4. What is one product you've made or service you've provided in the past that has made at least one person very happy? Try to come up with at least a few ways in which you could turn it into a product-oriented business and use it to provide a service. Do you think you could do both under the roof of one business?

Here are just some of the more popular businesses in both the service- and product-oriented arenas, including some you may not have even thought about.

Service-Oriented Businesses

• Manicurist

• Financial planner

• Computer technician

• Dog groomer

• House sitter

• Genealogical researcher

Product-Oriented Businesses

• Any kind of retail store

• Craftsperson

• Import/export business

• Business supplies

• Specialty food producer

Some Businesses That Are Both Service- and Product-Oriented

• Restaurant (serves meals and sells prepared and packaged foods)

• Inn, Bed & Breakfast (provides a bed and a meal or two, but can also sell products provided for guests at the inn, like mugs, robes, and cookbooks)

• Consultant (gives seminars and privately troubleshoots for businesses and individuals, but can also sell books, tapes, and other material based on his knowledge)

Research Upcoming Trends

There's a big difference between a trend and a fad. Though it is possible to start and then grow a wildly successful business that revolves around a fad—think Hula Hoop, Pet Rocks, and yes, Beanie Babies—these products tend to burn hot and fast and therefore usually extinguish themselves before a year or two has passed. The upside is that you can make a lot of money in a short period of time, which you can then use to start another business, preferably one with more staying power. The downside is that it's virtually impossible to predict which products will develop into the full-blown fads that will have every American kid and adult clamoring for them.

Though it's nice to dream about striking it rich, developing a fad is akin to winning the lottery. Most aspiring entrepreneurs realize that they're better off selecting a business that takes advantage of trends that may start off slowly, but will be around for the long haul, changing along the way and therefore creating even more markets in which to sell to a current and loyal customer base.

One important development to be aware of, and one that will be touched on a number of times in this book, is that the American economy has switched from its long-standing roots as a manufacturing-based economy to one in which businesses that provide services prevail. This trend is only bound to continue to grow, and anybody who's looking to start a new business had better take this into account since manufacturing jobs are becoming scarce, as large and small companies have found they can save significant amounts of money by sending some of their jobs overseas.

However, at least one aspect of the manufacturing economy is growing in the United States. Companies that manufacture products the way they *used* to be made—with painstaking attention to detail, an eye towards the craft of the item, and the hand of a skilled craftsman—are growing as their quality becomes glaringly apparent when placed next to the mass-marketed products that most Americans buy. In other words, entrepreneurs who wish to start a business producing handmade furniture, boats, or other finely crafted items will thrive . . . in part because the thriving service economy has brought great wealth to many Americans who are able to afford these hand-crafted, rare items. So as the number of service-oriented businesses grow, so will these specialized manufacturing companies, which often begin as a one-person home business.

When you start to research upcoming trends to make sure that your business will fit right in and

SMART SOURCES

If you've never heard of The National Association for Storage Executives, you may be unaware of the wealth of trade organizations that serve business owners.

One of the best resources for trade publications and industry associations is *The Encyclopedia of Associations*, a mammoth five-volume reference work that lists almost every association—for businesses, social groups, nonprofits, and others—in the country. Published by Gale Research, it typically costs $550 for the set, but most public libraries have copies in their reference sections.

If you can't find it, pick up a copy of the current *Writer's Market* and flip through the list of trade magazines in the back—the variety is a real eye-opener.

begin planning the shape that your business will take, consider the following questions and suggestions.

Self-Assessment Quiz 4

1. Are there other businesses already doing what you would like to do? If so, how long have they been around? And have they been largely successful?

If there isn't already a business filling the niche that you plan to fill, don't fret. It may mean that you have a special talent for keeping your finger on the pulse of American life, but it may also mean that your idea is just a little ahead of its time. Sometimes being second in a given field is better than being first; if you're providing a brand-new product or service that people haven't previously viewed as necessary to their lives, educating these people about the need for your business can eat up huge chunks of money. And if you don't have deep pockets, watch out. Just about the time that people are catching on to your message, your funds may be depleted and you have to close your doors. But if you're second in line after the first guy runs out of money, he's already done most of the expensive dirty work for you and, as a bonus, has left you without serious competition.

So if you have a truly new idea that will take some time for people to get used to, you may want to sit back and wait until someone else goes first. If it is a good idea and there's a definite need for it, it's nearly inevitable that somebody besides you is considering it, too.

2. How are current trends affecting people who are already running businesses in your chosen field?

In businesses that are strictly non-technological in their origins, are the owners and managers continuing to dance with them who brung them, as the saying goes, or are they adapting their businesses in some way to take advantage of a whole new technologically-savvy audience?

Blue Mountain Arts started out as a greeting-card company back in the 1970s. The business thrived, but when e-mail and the ability to send a letter around the corner or around the world began to be measured in seconds instead of days or even weeks, the company started to take notice. They continued to do business as usual, figuring that no matter how many e-mails a person sends, they still need to send regular cards through the mail for birthdays and Mother's Day. However, they developed an additional segment to their business, offering Internet users the ability to send greeting cards as e-mail attachments with their own personalized greetings. The best part is that the company offered this service absolutely free of charge! The Web site provided the company with the ability to impress the name of the business upon people who used the site. So when people who had sent or received a Blue Mountain Arts card via e-mail saw the company's greeting card display in a retail store, some were more likely to purchase their cards than a competitor's since their previous experience with the company had been a pleasant one.

This is one example of a company that saw the writing on the wall when it came to rapid societal change, and decided to run with it, instead of from it. Try to think of some ways you could combine your business idea with a rampant popular trend in order to hit more market segments than you would otherwise be able to reach.

F.Y.I.

If you're considering a multilevel marketing business for your new venture, where you not only sell products but are also signing up people to sell products for you, keep in mind that some of America's most famous businesses are structured as MLMs: Avon, Amway, and Tupperware are a few.

SMART SOURCES

Trend forecaster Faith Popcorn has the CEOs at Fortune 500 companies eating out of her hand because of the crystal ball predictions she regularly makes about where Americans are headed in their business and personal lives. Whether it's the popularity of cocooning or sport-utility vehicles, both of which she predicted back in the mid-1980s, her predictions are so accurate to be frightening.

As you further refine your business idea, make sure to pick up a copy of each of Popcorn's books, *The Popcorn Report*, and *Clicking*. See what she has to say about the future of certain trends, and come up with ways that you can tweak your idea to fit these trends.

3. Are you coming in on the tail end of the trend? If so, are you prepared to rapidly switch gears or branch out when the market becomes saturated?

Remember all the bagel chains and upscale coffee shops that seemed to appear overnight? Investors and franchise purchasers hopped on the bagel bandwagon hoping to make lots of dough from a very popular product that only cost pennies to make. The same herd mentality was also evident in the sudden proliferation of coffee shops like Starbucks and Seattle's Best Coffee. Suddenly, in many cities, there was a coffee shop and a bagel place on every street corner. No matter how densely populated, no neighborhood can survive that kind of redundancy. As with other trendy businesses, after the saturation, a consolidation usually occurs, with the weakest ones getting run out of the jungle.

How to Scope Out the Competition

Just as family and friends scoffing at your plans to start a business can impel you to move forward, existing competition in your field can also provide enough motivation to keep you going in your business.

It's not necessary to hire a private investigator to scope out the competition; in many ways discovering facts about the businesses you will be competing with can serve as an invaluable way to learn details about your business before you start. In fact, consider it to be a way you can learn from all the mistakes someone else has made.

Investigate businesses that are similar to yours, those operating locally and across the country. Call them or visit them in person and pose as a customer. Note everything you can about each business and ask the questions you think your own customers will be asking you once your business is up and running. It's possible to ask probing questions that will give you an idea of how serious a threat a business will pose to you, while nonchalantly playing the curious customer.

Depending upon how friendly you perceive the business owner to be—and how rushed he is at the moment—you can ask questions about how well business is going and what new ideas are being considered in order to increase business.

If you can test out businesses that are similar to yours, both direct competitors and those that are outside of your circle of customers, you will be able to come away with information that will help you to focus the way you will run and market your business.

What Did You Learn?

Two important questions to ask yourself after you've completed the interrogation: First, what do you like about the way they run their business? Second, what is one thing you noticed about their business that you would never use in your own? Remember, if you're entering an area where your business will be facing competition, as long as you can focus your business in a way where you're doing something that your competitors are not, you have an excellent chance to make your business stand out despite the competition.

Another way to scope out your competition is to notice the changes they experience over a period of time. If you're thinking of starting a magazine, for instance, look at a full year of back issues of your closest competitor. Is the current issue carrying significantly more ads than a year ago? Do certain times of the year result in issues that are thinner than others? If you could take over the business, what would be the first changes you would make?

Your discoveries will go a long way in establishing your own customer base while rightfully winning some followers from your competitors.

Will It Fly?

This may be the hardest question for an aspiring entrepreneur to answer when it comes to her new baby, her business. "Of course it will fly!" she replies, indignant that anyone would doubt her ideas as well as her intelligence.

Here's the hard truth: Four out of five businesses that are around today will no longer exist five years from now. There are certain industries that have an even greater mortality rate, among them restaurants and retail stores, which ironically, are two of the more popular businesses to start.

By no means should you be discouraged from following your dreams. On the contrary, by reading this book you've taken a serious first step toward long-term success by carefully planning your business instead of starting it in a haphazard way.

Researching the need for your business as well as envisioning how it will fill that need is the single most important task you can do to ensure that your business will make it to its fifth birthday. In doing so, you're taking bigger and wiser steps than do the majority of people who start their own businesses.

Evaluate Your Resources

One of the first questions you should ask yourself is if you will be able to run and manage your new business with the resources you'll have at hand. For example, if your budget projects that you won't be able to hire help for the first three months, and you plan to work six full days a week by yourself to be available to serve customers, when will you find the time to do the bookkeeping, recordkeeping, marketing, and all of the other little but very necessary behind-the-scenes aspects of running the business? Will your spouse take care of these responsibilities? Or do you plan to get around to doing them when you have some spare time? Here's a hint: Once you start a business, the concept of spare time will become a fuzzy but pleasant memory.

Put It In Writing

Some people feel that if they don't write something down they want to remember later, it's as good as gone. Successful entrepreneurs know that if they don't develop a detailed plan in which they list all the myriad responsibilities of running a business, they might as well not start the business in the first place. You will be able to address the details of planning your business in chapter 3, "The Best-Laid Plans." Here is where you will concen-

WHAT MATTERS, WHAT DOESN'T

What Matters
• Being nice to your competition. Despite the tales you hear, the owners of many competing businesses are cordial with each other.

• Talking to people about your business before you open your doors. You'll get invaluable feedback.

What Doesn't
• Risking your health, sanity, and relationships with family and friends for a business that shouldn't have been started in the first place.

• Being a slave to trends. Don't trash your business idea if it doesn't happen to tie in with anything that's currently big. It's the day-in, day-out stuff that's the bread and butter of American businesses.

trate on getting as much as you can down in written form.

But before you even type out the title page for your business plan and start to consider where you want to invest your time and money, you'll need to know if you'll be able to handle the business with the warm bodies you've allotted to your business at start-up. Does it sound too good to be true that you'll be able to play Superman or Superwoman seven days a week, without a break for yourself or your family? Are your plans just a bit ambitious for the early days of your business?

If so, it may be a good idea to start your business part-time at first, instead of the full-time schedule you had envisioned, or start your business at home instead of renting an outside office. As recently as 1995, entrepreneurs who ran their businesses from home offices used to disguise this fact. Some still do, but far more make it a point to flaunt it, since home entrepreneurship has since become the rule and not the exception.

Here's something else for you to consider: what if your business takes off beyond your wildest dreams from the very first day? Though it may mean more revenue to work with, it still may mean no additional salary for you, and it may mean a lot more headaches if you expand quickly without figuring on additional help to get the work done. More importantly, does one of your ultimate goals include running a business with hundreds of employees, several branch offices, and with you spending your time managing people instead of doing what you went into business for in the first place?

Though it's a nice thing to dream about, you must be realistic about your goals. But here's one truth for every beginning entrepreneur: Once you get a taste of what it's like to run your own business, your life will never be the same.

After Laying the Groundwork . . .

You've started to lay the groundwork: The site is prepped and the cement mixers are ready to go. But wait! Where are the plans?

Many people believe that taking the time to develop a business plan will just slow them down.

They're wrong.

Planning a business is a vital step in starting a business. And it's not that bad . . . you'll see in the next chapter.

THE BOTTOM LINE

Patience is a virtue, and usually a very foreign concept to entrepreneurs who feel it's necessary to pounce on an idea *now* in order to beat the competition.

Calm down. Once you decide on a specific business and a particular niche, let it marinate while you start working on all the other details involved in starting your new venture. Selecting your business and narrowing down your niche are two things you shouldn't rush. Remember, even though being an entrepreneur is a good thing—look at Martha Stewart— starting the wrong business could sour you on being your own boss and on the rewards that will eventually come your way.

CHAPTER 3

The Best-Laid Plans

• It's necessary to select a legal business structure—sole proprietorship, partnership, or corporation—that fits your particular business and spells out the ownership of the enterprise.

• Licenses, permits, and trade-name registrations are all part of planning a business, though regulations often differ by state and type of industry.

• It's important to assemble a panel of lawyers, accountants, and consultants who you can call on for professional advice.

• Your business plan is where you will keep all of the details, plans, forecasts, and financial data that will help lead you through the early days of your business.

Yes, it's a cliché, but clichés hit home for a reason so listen closely:

You probably would not set out on a long road trip without a map, but running your business without a plan would get you just as lost.

Even if you're the adventurous type, believe me your business will provide you with plenty of excitement; you don't need the stress that comes from a hastily executed, sloppy form of attack.

Keep in mind that the sooner you attend to the details of starting up a business the sooner you can get right to the good stuff: working with customers, creating a product, or providing a service that you absolutely love.

Spend some time to arrange the nuts and bolts that are necessary to support your business and organize your workspace, so that you will be able to spend more time doing the things you love—and not backtracking to set up your bookkeeping system long after you needed it, or spending hours searching for an important piece of paper. Think of it this way: The planning techniques covered in this chapter are the best way to set up your business so that you will be speaking a common language with other businesses, suppliers, and professionals, all who have a vested interest in helping you to succeed.

Business Structures

Every business, large and small, falls under a particular form of business structure: **sole proprietorship, partnership, corporation,** or **limited liability company.** Federal and state governments, as well as the

Internal Revenue Service, will treat you differently depending upon the kind of business structure you choose. Each has its own advantages and disadvantages, and one form may be a better fit than another for specific businesses and industries.

One of the most common factors that influence the choice of one structure over another is taxes. Your tax bill will differ, depending upon whether you're a sole proprietorship or a corporation, as will the frequency and methods in which you pay your pound of flesh. Profits and liability issues are also directly affected by your business structure.

It's important to be familiar with the various kinds of business structures because, even though you may already know which is best for the business you're about to start, it's possible that you may want to change your structure in the future, particularly if you're starting out as a sole proprietor, which is the structure that many new business owners and solo operators choose. Even if you start out as a corporation, once you successfully build your business and then sell it, the next enterprise you start may need a simpler structure.

Sole Proprietorship

Essentially, a sole proprietorship is a **business that is owned by one person**. This is the easiest type of business to start, and the one that most solo entrepreneurs select to get off the ground. A sole proprietorship also requires a minimum of time to start, since the most you have to do is to register with your state government as a new enterprise by purchasing a business license. Once you have it in hand, you're off and running.

SMART SOURCES

There are untold numbers of publications and computer programs on the market that loudly proclaim that theirs is the best there is when it comes to informing aspiring business owners how to develop, write, and put together a business plan. To date, however, the most concise guide and the one that demystifies the entire process in plain English is *The Business Planning Guide* (Upstart Publishing) by David Bangs. Frequently used as a resource in classes run by the Small Business Administration, the book spells out the process of writing a business plan from start to finish and gives the reader the confidence to tackle the project. You know all those stupid questions you have but are afraid to ask because you're afraid you'll sound too stupid? They're all answered right here in this book.

Opting for a sole proprietor structure makes the most sense if:

• You are running your business by yourself or with only a few employees

• You don't plan to take on any business or financial partners

• The business you choose is a low-risk venture when it comes to the possibility of getting sued by either a customer or supplier

Your Liability

If you're running your business from your home and clients aren't required to visit your premises to conduct business with you, your current homeowners' policy or a simple business policy will more than likely cover you for liability. Of course, to be safe, you should check with your insurance company to make sure.

If someone does choose to sue you as a sole proprietor, because you are personally responsible for your business, the litigant can go after your home and all of your personal property because the sole proprietor structure does not differentiate between personal and business property: the law basically views you and your business as one and the same, making all of your property—house, automobiles, furniture, monetary investments—fair game.

Along the same lines, if your business should fail, leaving outstanding debts and loans, you are personally liable to pay off those debts even though they were generated by the business. In the past, people operating sole proprietorships found it more difficult to secure significant financing for their ventures than if their businesses were partnerships or corporations. In recent years, though, as more new businesses fall under the umbrella of sole proprietorship and prove to be solid business risks, banks and finance companies alike have loosened the borrowing reins.

Pros

• A sole proprietorship is easy to start; all you need is a business license.

• You are truly your own boss, not an employee.

• You can determine your own salary and benefits package, as well as receive tax breaks for some of your personal expenses, such as a home office and travel deductions.

Cons

• You are your business; if you are sued, your personal assets are liable as well as your business property.

• All debts are your personal responsibility.

• It may be harder to get approved for business loans since your personal credit is a factor in the eyes of a banker.

Partnership

A partnership is best described as **two sole proprietorships that have been combined into one.** More technically, however, the government regards a partnership as an "association of two or more persons to carry on as co-owners of a business for profit," as stated in the Uniform Partnership Act, which has been written into law in most states.

Because the issues of ownership and successorship (that is, who decides who runs the business if one partner wants to leave, or dies) are by necessity thornier in a partnership than in a sole proprietorship—twice as many owners means at least double the complexity—state governments have deemed it necessary for people going into a partnership to spell out how decisions will be made should the individuals not be able to agree on a particular issue. If only two people entering into a marriage were required to sign the same type of agreement!

The Articles

This document is known as the Articles of Partnership, and it basically serves as a miniature version of a business plan, dealing solely with the ties between the partners. It details the responsibilities of the partners and provides pre-agreed solutions to problems that may arise later. Though you can purchase a preprinted Articles of Partnership in a stationery store or have a lawyer draft one up, it's easy enough to write one yourself. Here's what the document should contain:

• The names of the partners

• The type of business formed by the partners

• The location of the business

• Details of the authority and responsibility each partner has in the business; whether one has final say over the marketing budget or another gets to choose the attorney used for legal issues faced by the business

• Details of the contributions each partner brings to the business, given as a percentage of the initial and/or ongoing investment capital; the number of hours worked each week; the contribution of a workspace; and other agreed-upon aspects

• A description of the favored accounting method for the partnership and whether it's paper-based or on computer

• Details of how business-related bills will be paid

• Salaries, bonuses, and commissions paid to each partner, and how and when they will be disbursed

• Details of how profits and losses will be spread among the partners

• Plans for altering the partnership, whether through a buyout plan, dissolution of the partnership, adding additional partners, or exigencies if one partner dies

• Details on how disputes will be moderated

If you form a partnership, it's important to explore how insurance requirements for the business will differ from those of a sole proprietorship. Check with your insurance provider to make any necessary changes before the Articles of Partnership is signed and notarized.

Pros

• Two heads in business are usually better than one, since there's someone else to bounce ideas off and to lend a different perspective.

• Frequently, the skills and talents of partners complement each other.

• Decision making is easier and quicker than for a corporation.

Cons

• Despite a formal agreement, if one partner skips town, the other is liable. One of the partners must assume personal responsibility for all debts and legal liabilities for the business.

• A partnership is only as strong as the communication and relationship between the partners.

• Banks and other financial organizations must use the personal credit history of at least one of the partners to approve loans or other financing.

Corporation

A corporation is a business structure that is organized through the authority of the government of the state where the business is located. It is distinguished from a sole proprietorship or partnership by issuing incorporation papers and capital stock in the company, which individuals or businesses can purchase, therefore making them stockholders in the company.

In simplest terms, a corporation is a kind of inanimate object that operates in a totally independent manner from both the people who formed it and the stockholders. In short, a corporation has its own needs and requirements that are separate from those of the individuals who run the company. If the company is sued by an individual or by another business, the corporation is liable, not the employees or board of directors. And even though you may have been instrumental in starting the business, you become an employee of the corporation, not an owner; a corporation can only be owned by the individuals who hold stock in it.

Because a corporation is its own entity, it has its own unique requirements when it comes to paying taxes and fulfilling legal obligations. In fact, corporations come under more federal, state, and local restrictions than do either a partnership or sole proprietorship. In this way, both growth and expansion as well as merger opportunities are more severely governed than for companies that fall under another kind of business structure.

Under the definition of a corporation, however, there are several different options to choose. If you're thinking about incorporating, it's a good idea to talk to an attorney as well as an accountant about the form that would benefit your business the most.

Pros

• Liability is limited in case of a lawsuit.

• If a corporate officer or founder is disabled, the corporation continues.

• It's easy to sell ownership in a corporation with the transfer of stocks.

SMART DEFINITION

C Corporation

A corporation that pays a tax on all income. Dividends that are distributed to shareholders are also taxed.

Sub-Chapter S Corporation

A corporation that does not pay a tax on its income; instead, the shareholders pay corporate tax, and they can deduct any losses that the corporation experiences.

Cons

• It can be difficult and expensive to start a corporation.

• The charter granted by a state may limit the type of industry in which a corporation may operate.

• Corporations are subject to double taxation, with corporate net income, and the paying out of stockholder salaries and dividends.

Limited Liability Company

A limited liability company (LLC) is a new form of business structure that is slowly catching on in this country among people who want the benefits of limited personal liability that a corporation offers without the number of restrictions. In addition, any profits or losses a LLC shows over its fiscal year are passed along to the owners of the LLC, who are usually referred to as members.

A LLC more closely resembles a partnership than a corporation, and accordingly, the Internal Revenue Service treats LLCs as a partnership. However, it is similar to a corporation in that it is required to issue stock; where the two structures part ways is that an LLC can issue more than one class of stock—for voting and nonvoting members—while corporations are limited to just one class that allows all stockholders to vote. In addition, while an S corporation requires all stockholders to be U.S. citizens, an LLC doesn't place such restrictions on its holders.

In short, an LLC is a business structure that contains the tax advantages of a partnership with the limited personal liability of a corporation. But it's not for everyone: businessowners tend to select an LLC over another form of business when none of the others quite fit the company's individual requirements.

Pros

• An LLC allows an unlimited number of stockholders, unlike an S corporation, which is limited to a maximum of 35.

• A partnership and traditional S corporation can be converted into an LLC.

• LLC income is taxed once, unlike a C corporation, which is taxed twice.

Cons

• LLCs are currently legal forms of business in all states except Vermont and Hawaii.

• Each state interprets the legalities of an LLC differently.

• An LLC is still a relatively new form of business that is both untested and unknown to clients and customers you may conduct business with.

SMART MONEY

Before you write out a check for any local permits or licenses, check with the local Small Business Administration (SBA), your city government, or the economic development corporation for your state to see if they have a special fund to help pay or at least defray the cost of applying. Frequently, because new businesses mean new employees and taxes, city and state governments—and even nonprofit foundations—will bend over backwards to help attract entrepreneurs. It may also be possible to convince a commercial landlord to absorb your fees as a cost of doing business, in much the same way he would pay for fixtures and renovations if you sign a long-term lease.

The Long Arm of the Law

Standardized tests. Sharpened number two pencils. Fill out this form within three minutes flat. Dealing with the legal aspects of starting a small business is almost like being back in grade school complete with the aroma of library paste and the irritation of chalk dust.

Wait! Don't give up! This next planning section is probably the most distasteful you'll have to deal with in starting your business because it involves filling out forms, paying fees, dealing with archaic governmental regulations and unenthusiastic civil clerks, all in an effort to make sure that your business will comply with a dizzying slew of laws, articles, and obscure legislation that sometimes seem like they have absolutely nothing to do with small business other than to discourage people from starting one. That is, if they've gotten this far.

It wouldn't be a great surprise to hear of aspiring entrepreneurs who changed their minds about going into business once they were face to face with a mountain of legal forms and licensure papers. Be assured, however, that this is probably the most tedious step in the entire business planning process.

To get started on your quest, first call your town clerk to see what you need to do to make your business legal on a local basis. The clerk will also be able to lead you to state offices so you know what you'll have to do with the state government.

Here's a rundown on some of the things you'll have to take care of in order to start your business off on the right foot.

Claim Your Name

The first thing you'll need to do is to register the name of your business with the state to make sure that the name you choose to do business under is not already being used by another company in the state. In most cases, you'll need to pay a fee for a business certificate. Not only does this establish that yours is a bona fide business, but it will alert state officials to expect to receive appropriate tax revenue from your business; if you don't pay, they know where you are . . .

Protect Your Trademarks

If you're manufacturing a product and you're worried about copying or infringement by a competitor, you can register the name as a trademark with the United States government. Trademark law is particularly complex, and it's not always required in certain cases, so before you spend a lot of money and time, you should check with a lawyer who specializes in trademark and patent law to see if securing a trademark or copyright is necessary for your business.

Check Your Zoning

If you're running your business out of your house, you'll need to check that local zoning laws allow for home businesses. Though millions of people are running businesses from home without their neighbors even being aware of it, many cities across the country prohibit home businesses due to anti-

STREET SMARTS

Frequently, the best consultant may be right under your nose.

That was certainly the case with the brother-and-sister team of Kenny Munic and Staci Munic Mintz, who founded Little Miss Muffin, a bakery specializing in wholesale accounts, in Chicago, in 1993.

They cut their teeth in the industry by working in restaurants owned and operated by their family. When they started the bakery, they rented space from their father in one of his restaurants for the first year. The primary reason they did this was to grow slowly and rent their own space when they could afford it, since they made it a rule to finance current operations and growth from existing cash flow.

But they also had a bevy of experienced consultants who were always around, at the ready to answer their questions.

quated laws passed when the vast majority of businesses—home or otherwise—were industrial in nature. Happily, many towns and cities are adapting and/or eliminating these restrictions on home-based businesses in response to local demand.

Conform to Code

The Americans with Disabilities Act requires that any entrance or exit to business offices and retail stores provide access to all people, regardless of physical handicaps. There are exceptions as well as differences depending upon the accessibility laws in your own state. But overall, federal law states that businesses with fewer than fifteen employees are exempt from complying with the law.

Your business may need to meet certain septic and water-use requirements if a health inspection determines that your existing systems will not be able to support the increased usage that employees and customers will place on them.

Get an EIN

If you plan to hire employees, you will need to apply to the Internal Revenue Service for an Employer Identification Number, which is basically a Social Security number for your business. As a business, you are responsible for making Social Security tax payments for your employees to the federal government. You will also be required to meet the standards of minimum wage regulations as well as workplace safety laws set by the Occupational Safety & Health Administration. And you'll need to contact your state Department of Labor and/or Employment Security to fill out the necessary forms to pay state unemployment tax, disability, and state income taxes for each of your employees. While you're at it, you should find out about worker's compensation insurance as well.

Register to Collect Sales Tax

If your business will be involved in selling merchandise and if your state has a sales tax on merchandise, you will be required to collect state sales tax, so you'll need to apply with the state tax commissioner for a resale tax number.

See If You Need a License

Depending upon your line of work, you may need to apply for a specific occupational license from the state board of consumer affairs, which is most often required of professionals like beauticians and CPAs. You may also need a permit to handle flammable materials, a food-service license, or others. Check with the state association for your particular field for the specific licenses and permits you will be required to carry.

Getting Professional Advice

When you're running your own business, though it may seem like the best thing to appear as a know-it-all in front of customers, suppliers, and anyone else who views you as an expert in your field, when it comes to the behind-the-scenes stuff, admitting that you know what you don't know is the best form of insurance you could carry for your business.

If you want to open a restaurant, you may have a recipe for the world's best lasagna tucked away in your files, but if you assume that your knowledge about the legal issues affecting your industry equals the extensive cookbook in your head, you'll be in trouble long before you dish up your first order of Fettuccine Alfredo.

When it comes to gathering up professional advice for your business, the hourly rates for attorneys, accountants, and consultants may seem far too expensive, but depending upon the advice you need and are given, it's far cheaper to pay for this advice—after all, you are buying a good deal of experience and expertise—than to take the time to learn about complex regulations by trial and error, which may end up with your doing something illegal without knowing it. Besides, getting legal and accounting advice ahead of time will save you a great deal of time that you could spend on growing your business.

The Small Business Administration

One of the frequently overlooked and most valuable sources of information and advice for both aspiring and experienced entrepreneurs is the Small Business Administration, a government agency whose goal is to help small businesses in the United States to prosper and grow.

The agency accomplishes this in a number of ways. One is with courses, seminars and information sessions designed to educate people in accounting, marketing, and many other areas especially important to small businesses. The SBA also makes much of this information available in publications and videotapes.

The Service Corps of Retired Executives (SCORE) is an SBA-affiliated association that matches up experienced retired executives with aspiring and experienced business owners who need counseling on running their businesses. To reach the national office, call (800) 634-0245.

Other services offered by the SBA are loan-guarantee programs, Small Business Institutes—which are partnerships between the Administration and local colleges—and regional Business Development Centers. To reach the SBA Answer Desk, call (800) 8-ASK-SBA. For general information, point your browser to www.sbaonline.sba.gov. The SBA's U.S. Business Advisor Web site is another great link that will hook you up to the wealth of business information and advice available from the entire U.S. government, not just the SBA. Go to www.business.gov to get started.

Good Counsel

If you have any questions about the legal aspects of running your particular business, you shouldn't hesitate to consult an attorney. Of course you can ask a competitor or even consult with the national or statewide trade association for your industry, but interpretations of the law can be radically different with even a slight change in your business or personal affairs, so as to render what appears to be quite specialized legal advice to be toothless.

It's not necessary to keep an attorney on a steep retainer; just make a list of your questions as they pertain to the law, and schedule a meeting with a lawyer who has experience with your business, either on the phone or in person. Stress that you are starting a business and can afford only an hour or two of the attorney's time. If the lawyer balks or gives any impression of being long-winded, find another lawyer who is better suited for your questions.

If you are incorporating your business, or purchasing an existing company to run as your own, you probably will be better off hiring a lawyer to tend to the annoying little details that always seem to pop up when it comes to doing anything more complicated than filing for a business license. Besides, don't you have enough to do already in starting your business?

By the Numbers

It is prudent to meet with an accountant in the very early stages of your business start-up if you have any questions about the kind of business structure your business should assume: sole proprietorship, partnership, or corporation. Since every business owner's tax and income situation is different, in order to minimize the amount of tax you are required to pay for any revenue generated by your business, it's a good idea to examine the different business structures in order to see which one works best for your particular situation. And if you're thinking of buying a particular business, an accountant will also be able to examine the financial records of that business and advise you of its future worth as well as its solvency.

Whether you're starting a business from scratch or buying an existing business, it's best if you are able to locate an accountant who has some experience keeping the books of a business that is similar to yours. Again, you can ask your local or statewide industry trade association for recommendations.

Another way an accountant can help you set up your business is to advise you on the tentative operating budget you'll be developing and whether it is realistic given your industry, your experience, and your first-year-in-business status. An accountant will also recommend a variety of accounting methods and advise you of any peculiarities you should watch for in your state's tax code.

Consultants

Too bad there's no such thing as a Good Housekeeping Seal of Approval for consultants, since it seems that anyone running any kind of business can hang out a shingle these days that reads Consultant.

Even though the term has become so overused as to be almost meaningless, the truth is that a person who has experience in the business you plan to start can be an invaluable source of information about what you can expect, both in the early days and a couple of years or more down the road. You can hire a consultant in a number of different ways: Before opening your doors, you can schedule a question-and-answer session where you ask the consultant everything you need to know; you can provide the consultant with a blueprint of your plans, your budget, and your experience—in essence, a copy of your business plan—and then have her write up a detailed report telling you where to fill in the blanks regarding your goals or

WHAT MATTERS, WHAT DOESN'T

What Matters

• Air. Office air quality is extremely important. Now that you can control it, get a humidifier, dehumidifier or air conditioner—or whatever else you need.

• Light. Experiment with spotlighting the work area on your desk.

• Comfort. Don't skimp on comfort and adaptability even if your budget is tight.

What Doesn't

• Size. Many entrepreneurs have started out using a card table in a corner of the living room. If this is your situation, let it motivate you to grow your business.

• A room with a view. It can both be distracting and reflect unnecessary glare on your computer screen.

SBA Loans

The SBA also offers a loan guarantee program. It doesn't loan the money itself, but instead works with banks in your area to qualify you, work over your revenue projections, and then recommend you to the bank. The SBA offers a number of loan programs, including the Low-Doc and MicroLoan programs, which require a minimum of waiting time and paperwork, however, can make it easier for a business startup to get approved for a loan than if you were to apply for a traditional bank loan.

It's a good idea to check out local SBICs (small business investment companies) that are subsidized by the SBA and possibly by local economic development councils and corporations. If you intend to add employees to your company, an SBIC may look more favorably on your business than the SBA, since it's their business to encourage economic growth and employment in your immediate region.

specifying any trouble spots to be on the lookout for and what to do should they arise.

And after you've been in business for a while and have ironed out the wrinkles but have a brand-new list of questions that you could not have imagined before your first day of business, it's a good idea to bring the consultant back for another round of troubleshooting. You will not believe how much you learned in the first month of boot camp of your business!

To find a qualified consultant, your statewide or national trade association will often be a good source of referrals, but you can also contact some of the people quoted in articles in the industry publication you read. Sometimes, these contacts can be more valuable than bona fide consultants because it is obvious that they are out working in the field and they are probably more affordable. In fact, some may even be so flattered by your request to pick their brains that they may even provide their services at no charge!

Your Business Plan

Every business needs a business plan. As a matter of fact, even companies that have been around for a while and have never bothered to write one could benefit from having one.

A business plan is a road map, a blueprint that spells out the specifics of how you plan to grow your fledgling company. Although entire books have been written on how to write a business plan, as well as software developed to lead you by the hand, the truth is that the process is simple. It involves you stating on paper what you're going to do, how you're going to do it, and the time frame you plan to accomplish it in. Your marketing plan— a separate but equally important document covered in chapter 7—accomplishes much the same goal.

Though a business plan does not have to be a massively lengthy document, it does need to contain enough detail to answer the questions that a potential investor would likely ask.

But by no means should you refrain from writing a business plan if you aren't pursuing outside investors. Even if you're the only person ever to read the contents of your business plan, it will provide a yardstick that you can use to measure your progress, keep you on track with your goals and budget, provide you with a history of the founding of your business, and make it possible for you to follow a time line and project history.

After you write the first draft of your business

plan, set it aside for about a week. During that time, keep a notebook handy to jot down every idea—large and small—that comes to mind about your business. Then use this information to fill in the blanks in your business plan or add details where you haven't fleshed out a topic.

The following are the very basic points that are a necessary part of every business plan.

• **Front Matter.** A cover sheet, a statement of purpose (that is, what you hope to accomplish with your business), and a table of contents.

• **About the Business.** What product(s) or service(s) will the business provide to customers? Who is your target market? Where will the business be located? Who is the competition? What about the staff you plan to hire?

• **Financial Data.** Month-by-month income and cash flow projections for the upcoming year. If you are purchasing an existing business, the financial records from the previous twelve-month period, plus annual revenue streams and expense reports should be included for the previous two-to-five years of the business's operation. (For more information and examples of the financial details needed for a winning business plan, see chapter 5, "Money, Money, Money.")

• **Supporting Documents.** These should include all the records that prove the viability of the business and vouch for your character. Résumés of the founder(s), a credit report, letters of reference from past business colleagues, press clips touting previous business successes, and anything that you feel will help the reader get a good idea of what you plan to do with the business and why you're well-suited for the job.

If you are still resisting the idea of writing down all the odd tidbits and visions that are floating around in your head, probably because some evil-spirited high school English teacher was mildly entertained by the thought of you ever writing a coherent sentence, take heart in this:

Writing is a funny thing. Though most of us fight it, even professional writers, those early-grade-school experiences when our knuckles got rapped with a ruler for using the "wrong" word are more potent than we would like to acknowledge. You should attempt to put your hesitations aside, however, because the act of putting pen to paper—or fingers to keyboard—can reveal much more than you realize. You've seen it happen before: you begin to write a letter to a friend, intending only to ask a single question, and before you know it you've filled eight single-spaced pages with more questions, news, stories, and memories. The same holds true for your business plan: as you write, you will think of other ideas and projects and tasks that might not have floated up otherwise.

And remember it doesn't have to be fancy. Just write it down!

Get to Work!

Okay, so you have managed to get it all down in writing. Now it is time to roll up your sleeves and really get to work. While the information coming up in the next chapter still revolves around the topic of setting up your business properly, here is where it starts to get interesting—you will begin to start integrating the specifics that are unique to your business into the planning process.

Keep the momentum going: Every day you spend doing something to start your business brings you one day closer to your new life as an entrepreneur.

THE BOTTOM LINE

In order to be a successful entrepreneur, you have to start acting like one . . . now!

Actually, it's easier than you think. Just by laying the groundwork for your business, you'll quickly develop a fluency in your field that will have business-people and prospective customers automatically viewing you as the owner of a successful business.

Even if you have doubts about your ability to pull it off, do what all the positive-think gurus suggest to their followers: "If you want to change your life, start acting like you're already there."

After all, planning your business is not a dress rehearsal; it means you're already there.

CHAPTER 4

·····················

Tools of the Trade

Every business has a set of tools that are unique to its industry. But even businesses that are opposites in every regard share particular tools in common, among them bookkeeping methods, standards and protocols for dealing with vendors, and certain criteria to use when hiring employees.

Think of the points covered in this chapter as a way to learn a foreign language, the language of business. When you're done, you'll know how to talk about your business so that other entrepreneurs will know exactly what you're saying. And once you master these concepts, who knows what you'll be capable of accomplishing in your business.

Keeping the Books

Even if you hated math in high school, keeping a good financial record of every one of your business transactions—whether it's checks received or cash receipts for highway tolls paid while traveling on business—is a basic necessity. After all, every entrepreneur wants to know how much money her business is generating both before and after expenses, to see what all of her hard work is worth.

The good news is that with an abundance of inexpensive and comprehensive accounting software, the accounting tasks of a business are easier and take less time than ever before. These programs are so exacting that they allow you to see, for instance, the precise amount you spent on office supplies during the third week in August. If you can compare your revenue and expenses against the same period of time a month or a year ago, or against the figures in your business plan, you'll be able to catch expenses that exceed your projected budget and remedy them before they get out of hand.

Here's a list of some of the information that you'll want your bookkeeping system to provide you with on a daily, weekly, monthly, quarterly, and annual basis:

• Available cash on hand

• Balances of any business-related bank accounts

• Total of sales and/or cash receipts

• Total expenses (payroll, bills, petty cash, etc.)

• Total in accounts receivable (the amount of money your customers owe you) with details on the balance and how long they are past due

• Other information that will help you to keep financial track of your business

One benefit to making the time to enter the data into your records at least once a week is that it will be easier for you to compile annual figures at tax time. If you also file away paper copies of all your records to correspond with your computer files, not only will you save a lot of money on accountant's bills in the unlikely case of a tax audit, but you'll be able to show receipts that back up a specific deduction in response to an auditor's questions.

There are two different types of common accounting systems that you can use to track expenses and revenue for your business: cash accounting and accrual accounting.

SMART DEFINITION

Single-entry bookkeeping

When writing down your financial records, one entry is recorded for each transaction in your financial books, whether it's revenue or an expense.

Double-entry bookkeeping

For every financial transaction, you enter two records, a debit and a credit. Double-entry bookkeeping ensures greater accuracy with its checks-and-balances system than does the single-entry system.

Cash accounting is the simplest method, since income is recorded in your bookkeeping records in the month it is received, and not necessarily when the bank credits the money to your account, while expenses are recorded when the check is written, even if the expense was incurred in a different month and the check cashed in the month after you wrote it.

Accrual accounting is slightly more complicated, but this method provides a more accurate picture of the financial health of a business. Basically, income and expenses are recorded on the day they are posted to your business account, and not necessarily in the month that you received the revenue or wrote a check. This form of accounting is more detailed and requires a bit more time because the bookkeeper must pay attention to end-of-month peculiarities (such as when payroll falls on a weekend day), as well as the timetables showing when your bank normally credits your account with checks—and credit card charges, if your business accepts them—and debits it for checks you've written.

Most new entrepreneurs and sole proprietors opt for the cash accounting method, because the accrual accounting method tends to provide more details and require more time than most people need or have. But it's your call; your accountant will be able to help you with your decision.

Insurance

Running a business is risky business. Advice on how to make sure your company is properly insured against every possible hazard that may arise could alone fill a book. All business owners decide to take risks at one time or another as a matter of course, but when it comes to choosing insurance, some go all out and insure their business, facilities, employees, and even themselves against the most remote risks, while others buy the minimum amount of insurance, usually for catastrophic events only.

You probably fall somewhere in the middle of these two extremes. An insurance agent may say that having no insurance is the most expensive kind of all, but when he tells this to a new entrepreneur with big dreams and a small budget, he may be wasting his words. When the most common risks involve replacement costs that are less than the deductible, being fully covered may turn out to be sheer folly. However, remember the old adage: Penny wise but pound foolish.

With this in mind, here are the kinds of general business coverage that most insurance experts recommend for entrepreneurs who are just starting out.

Liability Insurance

This form of insurance will cover you if a client or customer, an innocent bystander, or even an illegal trespasser gets injured while on your business premises. The premium for this coverage depends upon the square footage of your store or office, as well as how often clients and suppliers visit your place of business, if at all. In the case of a home business, standard homeowner's insurance will usually include coverage for personal visits, not liability for business-related accidents and claims. You will have to notify your insurer that you are operating a business on the premises.

Most homeowner's policies will cover up to $2,500 worth of home-office equipment, even if you don't notify your agent that you're operating a business from a spare bedroom. Still, independent consultant William Popeleski had to absorb the entire loss when his brand-new $6,500 laptop computer was stolen from an airport baggage claim area. Although his homeowner's policy might have covered part of the loss if the computer had been stolen from his house, the theft occurred "off-site," and thus was not covered at all.

"I didn't pursue insurance as aggressively as I should have," says Popeleski. "There are so many details you have to focus on in running a small business that I learned the hard way you have to be on top of it."

Automobile Insurance

Two types of auto insurance are necessary if your employees will be driving a vehicle in the course of working for your business: auto liability insurance on all business vehicles, and nonowned auto liability insurance, which will cover an employee if he needs to drive his own car or a vehicle that is not owned by you or the business. You'll also need to get additional coverage for any tools or other goods that are transported in a business vehicle; a standard business policy won't cover cases of theft or damage.

Fire Insurance

This policy will cover any fire damage to business equipment, inventory, and to the physical building if you are the owner. If you rent, it may be a good idea to add fire liability insurance to your business policy, which would cover any fire damage to the part of your landlord's building that your business occupies. When choosing fire insurance, make sure you choose **replacement value coverage**.

The most inexpensive form of fire insurance is to regularly back up all of your computerized business files and data on a separate disk, and keep the extra files at another location. Keep in mind that insurance companies will not reimburse you for the actual value of lost data when it comes to your time or to the intrinsic value of the electronically stored information.

Workers' Compensation Insurance

In most states and in most industries, if you have employees, you will need workers' compensation insurance, which will provide death and disability benefits to employees and employees' survivors. If your state is one of the few that does not require you to have workers' compensation insurance, in the event that one of your employees is injured, your business is still liable. Many state governments offer workers' compensation insurance to employers through a state plan; these programs tend to be somewhat less expensive than comparable plans offered through traditional insurance companies and agencies.

There are many other kinds of insurance you may choose for yourself, your business, and your employees, but the following is a list of the most common types. In some states the government requires that businesses provide one or more of these types of insurance:

• Health and hospitalization insurance

• Life insurance

• Disability insurance

• Credit insurance

• Unemployment insurance

• Environmental impact insurance

• Bonds and surety insurance

• Internal theft insurance

F.Y.I.

The Independent Insurance Agents of America, a trade association, conducted a survey of 4,000 business owners who ran their businesses from a home office. The group found that 60 percent of the entrepreneurs lacked enough liability and property coverage for their businesses.

Taxes

Now for the fun stuff . . .

Here is where most entrepreneurs believe the form of business structure you choose—as explained in chapter 3—matters the most. Whether you are a sole proprietor, partnership, or corporation determines when, where, and how much Uncle Sam and your state or municipality will extract from your business.

Since each state has its own idiosyncrasies when it comes to calculating and then collecting tax, this section will deal strictly with the federal tax system because it is the same for every American who owns a business, no matter which state he lives in. The good news is that nearly every single penny you spend in the course of doing business can be deducted from your overall business revenue, which in turn will reduce the amount of tax you'll have to pay to the federal government. That means that every single item that you list on the monthly budget you'll develop in chapter 5 will contribute toward whittling down the final line on the federal tax return you'll fill out. A warning here: In most cases, equipment, capital improvements, and business vehicles are not totally deductible all at once, but either partially or in stages. So before you head out to purchase a brand new copier or computer for your business, check with your accountant to see when you'll be able to deduct it and in what amount.

Because you are a business owner, you have a dual role when it comes to taxes. On the one hand, you serve as a tax collector, taking payroll deductions for federal income tax, social security, and other taxes from your employees, taking sales tax from your customers, then turning them over to the correct government department. But you are also responsible for paying taxes that are based upon the revenue your business generates. These may include federal income tax, state income tax, and property tax; the list can be lengthy.

If you are a sole proprietor, after subtracting business expenses from business revenue, you'll figure the personal tax you owe on Schedule C, which you'll include with Form 1040, and file once a year. However, in addition to filing a 1040, a sole proprietor is required to pay an estimated tax—calculated from the previous year's total paid income tax—each quarter; this amount is then credited toward the actual tax you owe, which is calculated when you send your return to the IRS.

A partnership files a report of annual revenue and expenses with Form 1065, "U.S. Partnership Return of Income," but no tax is due with this form. Instead, each partner divides the profits or losses as specified in the Partnership Agreement described in chapter 3, and adds this information to Schedule E, "Supplemental Income and Loss," which they then file with their individual 1040 form.

Both kinds of corporations file tax forms once a year, and most forms must be received by the Internal Revenue Service by March 15. There are exceptions, but for most American corporations, this is the rule. The similarity ends there, however. A regular C corporation reports revenue and expenses on Form 1120, or the short Form 1120A. A subchapter S corporation files Form 1120S, but is not responsible for taxes on profits and doesn't receive a credit in the case of a loss. Instead, an S corporation splits the profits among each of its shareholders who then receive a Schedule K-1, which lists their share of the income. The shareholders then include this information on their individual 1040 Form along with Schedule E.

You still there? Business tax law can be complicated, even for a sole proprietorship, but the simplest piece of advice is this: The tax code is always changing on the federal, state, and local levels. Just because you were able to claim one kind of expense as a deduction last year does not mean you will be able to claim it next year. So do your homework. And caveat emptor.

Working with Suppliers and Vendors

Large international corporations have departments crammed full of people whose only responsibility is to buy, buy, buy for the company: office supplies, employee vehicles, computers equipment, phone service, travel . . . you name it, they buy it. Their titles are usually Buyer or Procurement Manager. They also keep track of what arrives when, where it is stored, and how long it will last.

To a new business owner, this is the consummate luxury. Not only do you probably wish you had someone to do all this for you, but you could probably use the same big budget, too.

Needless to say, the lack of money and help will probably mean that when you first start your business, you'll have to do all the work alone. Even if you run a business based on your knowledge and experience, you'll still need to get materials and supplies, find your customers, and provide the information in a form that is useful for clients.

Finding Them

So how do you locate the suppliers and vendors who will provide you with everything you need in order to run your business? That's easy. The best sources for supplies for your business are the brands or companies with which you are already familiar in your personal life: the warehouse office supply stores, online office supply catalogs, and even the cleaning supplies under your kitchen sink or at the local discount store. If you need items that are more business-related than you've required in the past, the Yellow Pages is a great resource for vendors in your region. A brief run-through may even give you ideas for other products and services that may help grow your business.

The advantage of working with these companies is that you can pick up the materials yourself whenever you need them, and there's usually no minimum order. The downside is the cost. Because you are not buying twenty-five boxes of copy paper at one time, you're probably paying a lot more. Plus, you either have to pay for the supplies when you pick them up or put the expense on your credit card, where you may then pay interest on the purchase. Of course, if you can deal with wholesalers and distributors from the beginning, you will probably be billed on a net thirty-days basis—payment due thirty days after you've accepted the delivery—and get free shipping, which can add a significant boost to your cash flow every month. But you don't need twenty-five boxes of copy paper . . . *Yet.*

And you probably don't have the storage space handy, either. Besides, the distributor might even decide that you're too small potatoes for him to deal with anyway. In any case, the question you'll regularly face when it comes to supplies is quantity versus price. Since you probably don't want to tie up a lot of money in materials you won't be using for several months, it's a good idea to pay the extra cost to get fewer supplies and be able to use your money for other business-related items.

Joining Forces

Another good source of suppliers when you're starting out is the list of vendors supplied by the local or national trade organization for your industry. When you join the National Association of Small Specialty Food Manufacturers, for example, you get a membership card and a subscription to the monthly trade publication, but most trade groups also provide members with a list of approved vendors. These are companies that have agreed to provide their service or product to members at a discount regardless of the quantity they need. They do this because it's a market they may otherwise not have tapped, and they're counting on you growing into a larger business, which will mean more business for them. When you place an order with an approved vendor, you will have to give your membership number, but that's usually as complex as it gets. You get the lower quantity you need at a price that's less than you'd be able to get on your own or at one of the superstores.

If you're not sure yet what different types of supplies and items you will need to successfully operate your business, take a look at the advertisements in the trade association's monthly publication. Note the advertisers you think you may need to call on in the future; you can even call them up to get a copy of their catalog and price list. And if there's a product or service you know you need but can't find a company to provide, call up your

trade organization and ask the membership services director for leads.

Later, as you grow, you'll want to deal with wholesalers and distributors and sales reps who will cater
to your business, offer free shipping and delivery,
and set up accounts for you at reasonable terms. But
as with everything, there are clear exceptions; in
fact, you may discover that all things considered, you
still get the best price at the same haunts you fre-
quented before you became an entrepreneur. No
matter what, once you set your priorities as to cost or
convenience, there are plenty of vendors and suppliers around who will be happy to bend over backwards to help your business grow.

Hiring Employees

Hiring a staff of employees, or even deciding whether to take on just one in the first place, can be
one of the most difficult decisions a new entrepreneur can make.

Labor (and all the associated costs: insurance,
additional equipment, supplies) and employer-
paid taxes turn the employment section of your
budget into your single largest expenditure. The
decision can also take an emotional toll. Becoming an employer means that you are responsible
for another person's livelihood. If your business
should suffer a setback, even a temporary one, the
fact that payroll is your largest single expenditure
may mean that you may have to lay people off in
order to save your business. And in good economic times or bad, letting an employee go is easily the most unpleasant part of being the boss. A
close second is the frequently overwhelming amount

of paperwork required by federal, state, and local governments for taxes, insurance, and other employee expenditures.

However, taking on employees so you can get more work done and grow more quickly is not the only advantage to hiring people. Since entrepreneurs are so close to their businesses they are sometimes unable to gain a clear perspective on pressing business problems; having access to another person who is familiar with the business and possesses a completely fresh pair of eyes can be a great help in those instances.

What Are You Looking For?

Before you write a help wanted ad or start asking people for referrals, you should make a list of the tasks you'd like your employee to handle. Does he need special skills? Do you need him full or part time? Is there special equipment he needs in order to accomplish the goals you set for him? Be reasonable about the amount of work you would need an employee to handle in the time frame you can afford.

What Can You Pay?

Next, you'll have to decide what kind of salary or hourly wage to offer. The best way to decide is to check the help wanted ads in the local paper to see what the competition offers to employees who hold jobs similar to the one you're looking to fill. Granted, businesses that are just starting out frequently cannot afford the salaries and benefits of a larger, more established company, so if you can find some way to compensate for the lower pay, do so. Some new entrepreneurs let their employees work at home part of the time, or allow them to choose the hours when they'll work. Many people who juggle family and work responsibilities will gladly take less money in return for being able to incorporate more flexibility into their lives.

Where to Look

How will you find employees? Your opportunities are limitless. Many companies advertise in their local newspaper, but some studies have suggested that newspaper ads actually bring in the smallest number of qualified applicants when compared with other methods.

Telephone your state's Department of Employment and have the organization place your help - wanted position on their online site and the office bulletin boards. Since the job placement specialists there already have applications from qualified people on file, they may be able to suggest a few candidates when you first call. Local college and school job banks have students who are willing to work part time or full time in the summer or upon graduation, and the good thing about hiring a freshly minted student is that you essentially have a blank slate—meaning that more than likely they won't come with any bad business habits you'd need to break.

Private employment agencies are also good sources for qualified candidates, but they tend to charge a hefty fee for the privilege—usually from 10 to 25 percent of an entry-level employee's first-year salary.

The Internet has proven to be a great source of technologically savvy, enthusiastic employees from all over the world. You can place help wanted ads on Web sites that cater to job seekers and with newspapers that place their help wanted ads online. News groups, mailing lists, and even personal Web sites can also serve as sources to fill jobs. If you have a Web site devoted to your business, you can add a page that describes the job and the type of applicant you're looking for.

Yet, hands down, the best source of employees tends to be people you already know, whether they're colleagues, coworkers from a previous job, or friends and family. Ask them if they know of anyone who would be a good match for the job that you have to offer, and then ask them to put the word out among their circle of friends, acquaintances, and coworkers.

Stay the Course

Whether the job market is tighter than a drum or people are lining up for jobs, your goal in searching for an employee shouldn't waver: you want the best-qualified candidates to consider for the position, whose aim is to help your business grow. Don't settle for a person who is less qualified than what you're looking for. However, if a qualified candidate comes along who isn't quite what you had in mind but is enthusiastic about your business and seems like a quick learner, you can temporarily adjust your requirements: reduce the pay scale, hire her on a probationary status, and challenge her in as many ways as you can to discover if she's the right person for the job. She may be so competent in one area that you may be willing to forego her lack of talent in another and take responsibility for it yourself instead. Just as employees cherish flexibility in a job, employers need to have a flexible attitude when it comes to their employees.

Managing Employees

The art of management once prescribed that a boss or manager should rule with an iron grip. Both employer and employee knew who was in charge. And the employee went along with these terms. But more often than not, the sly employee managed to get away with things whenever he could, did only what was expected of him, and never did anything more.

The opposite philosophy was that of the sensitive manager. He soft-pedaled harsh news, coddled his employees, and was always at the ready to heap lavish praise on even the tiniest of accomplishments. Again, employees went along with it, but felt they were never fully trusted or appreciated for their own talents and efforts. As before, quality and morale suffered.

Empower Your People

The ideal management style for a small business is to let employees feel as though it were their own and to give them a measure of responsibility for the business's successes or failures.

This style is perfect for business owners who need to delegate particular tasks and who work very closely with employees on an ongoing basis. This type of management may run counter to what many people think being a boss ought to be, but in the end, you'll find that your employees will be happier, more productive, and will also stay with you longer if you learn to manage them in this way.

It's not easy to do this, however. People who feel they have to control their employees in order to get them to work may run into problems with executing this altered style of management. However, once you see that your employees will treat your business almost as well as you do, it won't take long for you to become a proponent of this management style and actually begin to adopt it in other areas of your life.

The secret to successfully managing employees is to show them what to do, trust that they'll do it, and then to just leave them alone. Though many employees will be taken aback by this unique approach, and some will find it to be too alien for their tastes, the great majority will meet the challenge and help to build your business while cultivating a personal relationship with you.

What works best is to show your employee what the final result should look like, and then go off and do your own thing. As long as the basic quality of the job isn't compromised, it helps to learn to look the other way. Some business owners are perfectionists, however, and they think that no one but themselves knows how to do things the right way. Unfortunately, this kind of manager will find it hard to keep employees, and may be burned out by the end of his first year in the business.

Though you're still calling the shots, compromise and acceptance is the name of the game when it comes to managing employees and maintaining the steady growth of your business.

Using Independent Contractors

If you can't find exactly the kind of employee you want, you may decide to farm the work out on a contract basis, either to a business or an individual who freelances or moonlights for extra income.

The advantage of using independent contractors is that when times are tight employment-wise, you don't need to look far for help. The biggest plus, however, is that the two of you agree on a fee for the project, the contractor performs the work, you pay her, and that is the end of your commitment, unless you provide her with more work. This means that you are not responsible for calculating tax and insurance deductions from her paycheck or for sending them to the appropriate governmental agencies. As an independent contractor, she is responsible for figuring and paying her own taxes. This can save you a mountain of paperwork and a lot of time. You'll probably pay a little more to an independent contractor on a per-hour or per-project basis, but you'll save that and more in the time you'll spend on paperwork if the contractor was your employee.

If you pay an independent contractor more than $600 over the course of a tax year, you'll have to prepare and file a tax form known as a 1099, where you detail the exact amount of money paid out, along with the contractor's name, address, and Social Security number. When you do the taxes for your business, you'll then have to send a copy of each 1099 along with a Form 1096, listing the total amount your business paid to independent contractors.

The Internal Revenue Service has tightened up its definition of when an individual performing work for a business is an employee and when he is an independent contractor. If you have any doubts or questions, contact your accountant or the Internal Revenue Service to clarify whether an individual performing work for your business is in fact an employee or an independent contractor, and exactly what your tax responsibilities are.

Now That You've Got the Tools

Learning about the tools you need to run your business takes time, but it's another important step on the road to the first day you can fling your doors open and declare to the world that you're open for business.

First selecting your business, then making your plans, and now choosing your tools: What does everything you've read about up to now have in common? Like most everything else in life, it all requires money. How much do you need to start your business? Where will you get it? To find out, read on . . .

THE BOTTOM LINE

A well-equipped toolbox is essential for any business, no matter what tools are in it. Keeping your tools well maintained will help your business to run more smoothly. As an informed entrepreneur, it's also a good idea to stay aware of any new tools looming on the market that can improve your business, and therefore, your bottom line.

CHAPTER 5

·····················

Money, Money, Money

If you read enough interviews with top entrepreneurs and business owners, you'll find that the great majority will say, "I started with nothing when I started my business, and look where I am today." Whether it's true or not is, of course, another story.

But you should know that it's entirely possible to start your business on a single frayed shoestring and then build it into an international conglomerate. However, when it comes to these stories there are two frequently unvoiced footnotes: First, to reach the top, these successful entrepreneurs likely worked their tails off and were as frugal as possible. And second, when their businesses started to take off, they still acted, in most cases, like there was little or no money in the bank. Success in business is determined less by how much money you start out with—although it is indeed a crucial part—than by how you handle what you get once the business starts to fly.

Start-Up Costs

For many people, the idea of a business is ruled by the images that come to mind when they think of various companies they've worked for in the past. Unfortunately, it's this picture that most often intimidates new entrepreneurs who want to get their own businesses off the ground: either they think they need everything a larger, more established business has before they can open their doors, from fancy networked telephone systems to a professionally decorated office, and spend way too much to start, or they become overwhelmed at the amount of money they think they need to open their doors, and never do so because they figure they'll never be able to come up with that kind of money.

Of course, the amount of money you'll need for start-up costs will vary depending on the type of business you're starting, but there are certain across-the-board expenses that apply to most small business start-ups. The good news is that they are probably a lot less than you think.

Basically, you need to estimate what you'll have to do to make your business presentable to the first customer who walks through your door. In other words, you'll have to make your business look like a business. As a rule, service businesses require less money to start because you don't have to tie up your available, but limited, cash in inventory. There are exceptions, however, and partnering with distributors and wholesalers who will allow you to order parts and items as you need them—also known as just-in-time inventory—can help to minimize the amount of money you'll need to allocate toward start-up costs.

Using the business plan you developed in chapter 3 along with your own instincts as to what is the least you can do and the most you can afford, adapt the following list to start charting your start-up expenses, either in terms of a monthly payment or buying an item outright. If you already own the item—like a computer—put a zero in the space; this means you'll have more money to spend on the other categories.

Your Start-Up Expenses

Overhead

Initial rent and security deposit . . . . $_____

Facility improvements/decorating . . $_____

Computer . . . . $_____

Office equipment leases . . . . $_____

Office furniture . . . . $_____

Telephone/fax machine/voice mail $_____

Office supplies . . . . $_____

Product inventory . . . . $_____

Business licenses and permits . . . . . . $_____

Insurance . . . . $_____

Advertising . . . . $_____

Attorney fees . . . . $_____

Accountant fees . . . . $_____

Business stationery . . . . $_____

Miscellaneous expenses . . . . $_____

Total . . . . $_____

Once you've estimated your start-up costs, add up the total. Can you cut corners anywhere? Are you able to use the office equipment you already own? And is a state-of-the-art computer essential in the beginning, or can you borrow the year-old model your brother-in-law no longer uses? You'll discover that running a business is a continuous process of making choices among two or more options, like figuring if the higher-priced model will give you more for your money and if the lower-priced item provides real value while saving you a few real dollars. Figuring your budget in advance and deciding where you can cut corners is excellent practice for the day-to-day decisions you will encounter once you actually do start your business.

If you are finding it difficult to come up with concrete figures, put your best bloodhound skills to work. If you've received information on a specific trade organization, read the information, leaf through the magazine, and go onto the Web site of vendors to check the prices in their online catalogs. If you're having trouble making your list as concise as you can, remember the advice in chapter 2 for scoping out your competitors? Do the same thing, but this time do it with an eye toward looking for what they get away with, where it looks like they skimp and where they appear to invest more money.

Feel free to revise the figures as you collect more information and discover where you can possibly reduce your expenditures and where you will need to budget more money.

Your Operating Budget

In the course of running your business, you will have to deal with not one but two budgets: one for your business and one for yourself.

A business budget is also referred to as an operating budget, and it differs from the budget you developed for your start-up costs for several reasons: After operating your business for even a short time, you will have a much better idea of where the money goes, as well as what comes in. You'll also have some sense of when the money tends to arrive in your bank account, so you'll also know when you can expect to be able to pay your own bills.

F.Y.I.

Here are two simple formulas for keeping the basics of your operating budget in mind:

Sales =
Total Costs + Profit

or

Profit =
Sales – Total Costs

In other words, each dollar you receive in sales partially comprises the expenses required to run your business as well as profit from its operation. The second equation reminds you that whatever you have left over from your sales figure after paying your expenses—including your own salary, if you've budgeted for one—is considered to be profit.

Pretty simplistic, but these formulas will help you to continually question additions and increases to your operating bud-get, because without a profit, eventually you'll be without your business.

Even though you may know your market inside and out, you'll probably vastly underestimate the amount of money you need to launch your business. Dave Lyon and his family launched Uncle Dave's Kitchen, a specialty food manufacturer, in Bondville, Vermont in 1989. He secured start-up funds from friends and investors as well as an SBA-guaranteed loan from a local bank. "We asked for $250,000," he said, "but by the time the paperwork was done, we needed another quarter million."

They got the loan after being in business for only two years. "Our enthusiasm helped," says Lyon, "along with the fact that we had raised a quarter million on our own before that."

Essentially, a budget is a projection of the revenue and expenditures—and all the subsequent profit—over a period of time. A budget is usually structured to highlight the differences among each month's expense categories as well as providing a cumulative overview so you can see how much you've spent, for instance, on office supplies or rent over the course of a year. An operating budget should provide an entrepreneur with a sense of discipline when it comes to spending the business's money. In a way, an operating budget provides you with an at-a-glance snapshot so you can see how your projections are panning out and where adjustments—if any—are needed.

For instance, your fixed costs can't be changed, but if you're working constantly and productively, but still aren't generating enough cash to cover all of your expenses each month, a quick glance at your budget can help inform you to make one of several choices:

• Increase sales by raising your prices, selling more to each customer, expanding your market range

• Cut expenses by opting for part-time rather than full-time help, or reducing nonfixed costs

• Allow more time for the market to become aware of you, and wait out new purchases, improvements, and growth

Your Operating Expenses

None of these are easy choices, of course. But developing and then keeping track of your operating expenses will help secure a great future for your business and yourself.

Overhead

Salary . . . . $_____
Mortgage/rent . . . . $_____
Property taxes . . . . $_____
Insurance . . . . $_____
Utilities . . . . $_____
Heat . . . . $_____

Office Expenses

Telephone line . . . . $_____
Fax line . . . . $_____
Credit card commissions . . . . $_____
Postage . . . . $_____
Stationery . . . . $_____
Office supplies . . . . $_____
Printing . . . . $_____
Advertising . . . . $_____
Miscellaneous marketing fees . . . . . . $_____

Professional Expenses

Dues and memberships . . . . $_____
Accountant fees . . . . $_____
Attorney fees . . . . $_____
Independent contractor fees . . . . . . $_____

Office Equipment

Copier leases . . . . $_____
Computers . . . . $_____
Printers . . . . $_____
Software . . . . $_____

Company Vehicle(s)

Loan/lease payment . . . . $_____
Registration . . . . $_____
Insurance . . . . $_____
Gas . . . . $_____
Repairs/maintenance . . . . $_____

Employee Expenses

Payroll . . . . $_____
Taxes . . . . $_____
Insurance . . . . $_____
Workers' compensation . . . . $_____
Bonuses . . . . $_____
Employee discounts . . . . $_____

A Personal Budget

Although this is a guide to starting a small business, it's important to keep tabs on the money you spend on the personal side of the ledger. If you've never kept a budget for your personal life, now is the perfect time to start. You'll have to account for and keep track of every penny you spend in your business; doing the same thing when it comes to your personal life will help you to manage your money better all around. Plus, it will mean you'll have more money to invest back into your business; people who stick to a budget tend not to fritter away their money.

It's a good idea to prepare two personal budgets: one for how you live now, and one that you will use once you have started your business. For instance, once you start working at your own business full time, you may decide that you no longer need to spend $400 a month on new clothes, especially if you're going to be spending most of the day working at home by yourself. On the same note, the amount you budget for lunches out may be totally eliminated in your personal budget, but may increase in your business budget. After all, if you need to entertain current and potential clients over lunch, part of your restaurant tab can be treated as a business deduction; it's a good idea to check with your accountant to see the percentage you're able to deduct.

Your Personal Budget

Fixed Monthly Expenses

Housing . . . . $_____
Utilities (gas, electric, phone) . . . . . $_____
Food . . . . $_____
Car payment . . . . $_____
Transportation expenses . . . . $_____
Credit card payments . . . . $_____
Health and medical expenses . . . . . . $_____
Savings and investments . . . . $_____
Clothing . . . . $_____
Family expenses/childcare . . . . $_____
Student loans/education expenses . $_____
Miscellaneous . . . . $_____

Now add up the totals. Where can you comfortably cut expenses?

SMART SOURCES

If you hate looking at the numbers in your personal budget because you don't want to face the fact of all the stray dollars you've spent, it's time to get serious. After all, if you invested this "pocket change" into your business, the amount could mean the difference between operating in the black and closing your doors.

The best way to get a handle on your spending habits is with a comprehensive financial software program like Quicken, which will automatically categorize every one of your expenses—even chewing gum—and inform you as to the percentage of your total budget that each category takes up.

And Quicken also balances your checkbook, projects how much of any future raise you'll keep after taxes, and more.

Quicken
www.quicken.com

Money Terms

As you progress through this book, it may seem like you're spending a lot of time learning the basics of business lingo. And that's fine. As you continue to read, apply these basics to the real-world situations you expect to encounter once you start to run your own business. After all, you're more likely to be able to negotiate favorable terms with clients and convince a banker that you need a loan by using terms that everyone understands.

The information in your operating budget contains everything you will need to draw up the documents that are essential to the growth of your business. They are:

• Sales Forecast

• Cash Flow Projection

• Balance Sheet

• Income Statement, also known as Profit and Loss Statement

Sales Forecast

Trying to predict future sales is an inexact science at best, even for long-term entrepreneurs. For business owners who are just getting their feet wet, it can be downright maddening. How can you possibly predict your sales volume for the first month of business, let alone a year down the road, when so many variables will affect it, including your entrepreneurial inexperience?

The easiest—and most accurate—way to forecast future sales is with a simple chart that provides three different figures:

• Pie-in-the-sky figures, or the number that would be beyond your wildest dream, but still within the realm of the type of business you're running given your location, your time commitment, and other variables

• Catastrophic figures, or the amount of sales you could expect to gross if a flood, earthquake, and fire occurred all in the same month

• Somewhere in between, which may be the number you end up with when you add up the two previous figures and divide by two

Keep in mind that as the months fly by and you gain more experience running your business, you'll also start to learn what figures are realistic to expect. But it's fun to dream, and to have a goal. Think about the pie-in-the-sky figure. What would you have to do differently in your business in order to even come close to this number? Ask yourself this question regularly after you've been running your business for a while, and one day you may just reach those lofty heights.

Cash Flow Statement

Cash flow is the lifeblood of a business, since it symbolizes the steady movement of cash in and out of a company. With a cash flow statement, you'll be able to keep tabs on when you expect to receive revenue, or money owed you by customers, and

SMART DEFINITION

Fixtures

Fixtures are the parts of an office or storefront that belong to the landlord but can be used and changed by the renter. Fixtures include the electrical outlets, lighting, permanent shelving, and bathroom facilities.

Cash Flow Statement

Cash Flow Projections by Month, Year One

	Feb.	March	April	May	June	July
Cash Receipts						
Wholesale	$2,000	$4,000	$5,000	$6,000	$6,000	$6,000
Retail	$2,500	$2,500	$3,500	$4,000	$5,000	$6,000
Loan Sources	$30,000	$0	$0	$0	$0	$0
Total Cash Receipts:	$34,500	$6,500	$8,500	$10,000	$11,000	$12,000
Cash Disbursements						
Cost of Materials	$7,000	$7,500	$4,000	$4,500	$5,000	$5,500
Payroll Taxes	$0	$0	$4,000	$0	$0	$4,500
Marketing	$2,000	$2,000	$2,000	$2,000	$2,000	$3,000
Salaries	$3,600	$3,600	$3,600	$3,600	$4,800	$4,800
Advertising	$700	$700	$700	$700	$800	$1,000
Office Supplies	$300	$300	$300	$300	$300	$300
Shipping Materials	$200	$300	$400	$500	$550	$600
Insurance	$150	$150	$150	$150	$150	$150
Telephone	$300	$400	$400	$400	$500	$500
Miscellaneous	$40	$40	$40	$40	$40	$40
Postage	$800	$700	$750	$800	$800	$900
Loan Repayment ($30,000; 5 yr.)	$650	$650	$650	$650	$650	$650
Total Cash Disbursements:	$15,090	$15,690	$16,340	$12,990	$14,940	$21,290
Net Cash Flow:	$19,410	($9,190)	($7,840)	($2,990)	($3,940)	($9,290)
Cumulative Cash Flow:	$19,410	$10,220	$2,380	($610)	($4,550)	($13,840)

Aug.	Sept.	Oct.	Nov.	Dec.	Jan.	Total
$7,000	$7,500	$7,500	$10,000	$10,000	$12,500	$83,500
$7,000	$8,000	$8,000	$10,000	$11,000	$12,500	$80,000
$30,000						
$14,000	$15,500	$15,500	$20,000	$21,000	$25,000	$332,270
$6,000	$6,500	$7,000	$9,000	$9,500	$10,000	$81,500
$0	$0	$5,500	$0	$0	$5,500	$19,500
$2,000	$1,000	$2,000	$2,000	$1,000	$2,000	$23,000
$4,800	$4,800	$4,800	$4,800	$4,800	$4,800	$52,800
$1,000	$1,000	$1,000	$1,000	$1,000	$1,000	$10,600
$300	$300	$300	$300	$300	$300	$3,600
$700	$750	$750	$900	$925	$1,000	$7,575
$150	$150	$150	$150	$150	$150	$1,800
$500	$500	$500	$500	$500	$500	$5,500
$40	$40	$40	$40	$40	$40	$480
$900	$2,000	2,000	$2,000	$1,800	$3,300	$16,750
$650	$650	$650	$650	$650	$650	$7,800
$16,390	$17,040	$24,040	$20,690	$20,015	$28,590	$336,435
($2,390)	($1,540)	($8,540)	($690)	$985	($3,590)	($29,605)
($16,230)	($17,770)	($26,310)	($27,000)	($26,015)	($26,705)	

(Continued on page 100)

(Continued from page 99)

	Feb.	March	April	May	June	July
Cash On Hand						
Opening Balance	$2,000	$21,410	$12,220	$4,380	$1,390	($2,550)
(+-) Cash Receipts	$34,500	$6,500	$8,500	$10,000	$11,000	$12,000
(-)Cash Disbursements	$15,090	$15,690	$16,340	$12,990	$14,940	$21,290
Total=New Balance:	$21,410	$12,220	$4,380	$1,390	($2,550)	($11,840)

then manage this money so it is available when you need it to pay your bills. Getting the numbers down in writing will help you to figure which months you should stockpile extra cash, perhaps by postponing that renovation project you had planned, and which months you'll have enough revenue flowing into your checking account to reschedule it. Or you can plan to hold a special sale for the months when you believe you'll have more money going out than coming in; the discount you provide to your customers is worth it if your cash flow is positive instead of negative.

When working up the numbers for a cash flow statement, besides including standard expenses, like rent and utilities, you'll also count as expenses depreciation, amortization, and other situations which are technically expenses but don't directly involve cash that exits your business account. Although a cash flow statement could arguably be used to prove your business isn't doing so hot—after all, if you didn't include the depreciation on your computer and business vehicle in the projections, your cash

	Aug.	Sept.	Oct.	Nov.	Dec.	Jan.	Total
	($11,840)	($14,230)	($15,770)	($24,310)	($25,000)	($24,015)	
	$14,000	$15,500	$15,500	$20,000	$21,000	$25,000	$193,500
	$16,390	$17,040	$24,040	$20,690	$20,015	$28,590	$223,105
	($14,230)	($15,770)	($24,310)	($25,000)	($24,015)	($27,605)	

flow would look wonderful—as is the case with accrual accounting vs. cash accounting systems, the diligent use of cash flow statements provides a much more accurate picture of the financial health of your business.

A cash flow statement should be prepared and analyzed once a month.

Balance Sheet

A balance sheet is a financial statement designed to indicate the net worth of your business. Information about sales projections, revenue, and expenses are not included.

Instead, a balance sheet lists any and all assets as well as liabilities. *Assets* are defined as both *current*—accounts receivable, inventory, and all office supplies, anything that can quickly be converted to cash—and *fixed*, which includes business real estate, office equipment (owned outright or leased), and fixtures. The values of both current and fixed assets

When Pat Nottle of Emmaus, Pennsylvania, decided to open her own gift shop, she had next to no money. So she started with what she could afford, which was a tiny shop that she fixed up herself.

Not too unusual. But when it came to stocking her shop, called Patches, with the crafts, pottery, and other items she wanted to sell, she didn't make her purchases from wholesalers, she got most of her inventory by approaching craftspeople in the area, who arranged to sell their items on consignment. This was enough for Patches to gain a foothold and for Nottle to relocate to a larger shop in the same town.

Today, Nottle buys directly from wholesalers, but still sells merchandise on consignment.

are added together to provide a dollar amount of the total assets that are owned by the company.

Liabilities are listed as *current*—accounts payable, taxes that are due, and other loans or debts that will come due over the next year—and as *long term,* which includes all other debt like mortgages, multi-year vehicle leases, and agreements with other businesses or independent contractors with whom you have signed a contract for a term longer than one year.

A balance sheet is usually prepared on a quarterly basis for the first year you're in business, and then once a year after that.

Income Statement

An income statement is a simple document that can be prepared in a single keystroke with one of the bookkeeping software programs that also prepares invoices, balances your checkbook, and prints out checks. An income statement, also known as a profit and loss statement, is a document where you add up all given revenue over a stated period of time, and then add up all your actual expenses, or those that require cash to flow out of your business. Subtract the total expenses from the total revenue, and you are left with either a profit or a loss . . . that is, before any business tax you must pay (remember that payroll taxes are included in your income statement as an operating expense). Once you subtract the business tax, you are left with a net profit, or a net loss.

An income statement should be prepared at least once a month to keep track of the health of your business.

Sample Balance Sheet

Assets

Current Assets	$_____
Fixed Assets	$_____
Less Accumulated Depreciation	$_____
Net Fixed Assets	$_____
Other Assets	$_____
Total Assets:	$_____

Liabilities

Current Liabilities	$_____
Long-Term Liabilities	$_____
Total Liabilities:	$_____
Net Worth (total assets minus total liabilities or	
Owner's Equity)	$_____
Total Liabilities and Net Worth:	$_____

Finding the Funds You Need

Money is the oil that greases the often squeaky wheel of American businesses, large and small. While the primary ingredient of small-business success is hard work and lots of it, money is still essential to launch and then maintain the often-spotty first year of a small-business's existence.

Now that you have a good idea of how much money you need to start your business, and how much you'll need to generate to pay the bills every month, where are you going to find it? It's a sign of

Income Projections by Month, Year One

	Feb.	March	April	May	June	July
Sales						
Wholesale	$4,000	$5,000	$6,000	$6,000	$6,000	$7,000
Direct/Retail	$2,500	$2,500	$3,500	$4,000	$5,000	$6,000
Total Sales:	$6,500	$7,500	$9,500	$10,000	$11,000	$13,000
Cost of Materials	$5,125	$4,375	$7,000	$3,125	$8,000	$5,875
Variable Labor	$0	$0	$0	$0	$1,500	$1,500
Cost of Goods Sold:	$5,125	$4,375	$7,000	$3,125	$9,500	$7,375
Gross Margin:	$1,375	3,125	$2,500	$6,875	$1,500	$5,625
Operating Expenses						
Marketing	$1,000	$600	$2,000	$500	$4,000	$3,000
Salaries	$1,500	$1,500	$1,500	$1,500	$2,700	$2,700
Advertising	$650	$300	$300	$450	$900	$500
Office Supplies	$300	$300	$300	$300	$300	$300
Rent	$0	$0	$0	$0	$500	$500
Insurance	$150	$150	$150	$150	$150	$150
Telephone	$300	$400	$400	$400	$500	$500
Miscellaneous	$40	$40	$40	$40	$40	$40
Postage	$350	$400	$750	$600	$1,000	$2,250
Total Operating Expenses:	$4,290	$3,690	$5,440	$3,940	$10,090	$9,940
Other Expenses						
Interest (credit line)	$140	$140	$140	$140	$140	$140
Total Other Expenses:	$140	$140	$140	$140	$140	$140
Total Expenses:	$4,430	$3,830	$5,580	$4,080	$10,230	$10,080
Net Profit (Loss) Pre-Tax:	($255)	($705)	($3,080)	$2,795	($8,730)	($4,455)

Aug.	Sept.	Oct.	Nov.	Dec.	Jan.	Total
$7,500	$7,500	$10,000	$10,000	$12,500	$12,500	$94,000
$7,000	$8,000	$8,000	$10,000	$11,000	$12,500	$80,000
$14,500	$15,500	$18,000	$20,000	$23,500	$25,000	$174,000
$4,375	$11,625	$8,000	$10,750	$8,875	$12,625	$89,750
$1,500	$1,500	$3,000	$3,000	$3,000	$3,000	$18,000
$5,875	$13,125	$11,000	$13,750	$11,875	$15,625	$107,750
$8,625	$2,375	$7,000	$6,250	$11,625	$9,375	$69,250
$6,000	$1,000	$2,000	$2,000	$1,000	$2,000	$25,100
$2,700	$3,900	$3,900	$3,900	$3,900	$3,900	$33,600
$500	$600	$750	$800	$900	$1,000	$7,650
$300	$300	$300	$300	$300	$300	$3,600
$500	$500	$500	$500	$500	$500	$4,000
$150	$150	$150	$150	$150	$150	$1,800
$500	$500	$500	$500	$500	$500	$5,500
$40	$40	$40	$40	$40	$40	$480
$3,750	$2,000	2,000	$2,000	$1,200	$3,300	$19,600
$14,440	$8,990	$10,140	$10,190	$8,490	$11,690	$150,680
$140	$140	$140	$140	$140	$140	$1,680
$140	$140	$140	$140	$140	$140	$1,680
$14,580	$9,130	$10,280	$10,330	$8,630	$11,830	$152,360
($5,955)	($6,755)	($3,280)	($4,080)	$2,995	($2,655)	($83,360)

SMART MONEY

Sometimes even those who have spent their pre-entrepreneurial lives working in the field of finance have to get creative when it comes to raising money to start a business.

Today Arthur Lieb runs a thriving business as a personal financial consultant, but despite the fact that he served as the volunteer director of the federal credit union at the Library of Congress, in addition to his primary position as Executive Officer, he had to start from scratch to get his practice off the ground. Though setting up his home business required a minimum of cash, he had to perform pro bono work for his first few clients, to prove the value of his services. Lieb considers this work to be the primary monetary investment he needed to get his business off the ground.

a true entrepreneur to believe that your talents and energy levels are so wide-reaching that the cash will start pouring in—and never let up—from the first week your business is open. But even if this fairy tale were to come true, there are far too many contingencies and unexpected expenses to be able to comfortably rely on this for long. Another way is to use available cash to grow the business as it comes in, a kind of pay-as-you-go method. The problem with this technique is that if you're forced to rely on whatever comes in, or whatever's left over after you cover the basic expenses of your business and your personal life, the growth of your business can be spotty and sporadic, or nonexistent. Steady business growth relies on consistent effort and marketing, and if you plan a big advertising campaign one month, only to run out of advertising money for six months, your customers and clients to be may wonder where you've gone during your hiatus. Some may even think you've gone out of business, and call a competitor before they think to contact you to see if you're still around. Remember the tortoise: Slow and steady wins the race.

There are a variety of ways to find the capital you need for your new enterprise. Many new business owners use their own funds by liquidating savings accounts, stocks, bonds and other investments, or selling a house or other big-ticket item. While this may limit the projects and growth of a small business, the advantage is that because you're not pressured by outside investors or the necessity to meet a monthly loan payment, you will answer only to yourself and your own vision for your business, not to outsiders who may not be familiar with the quirks of your business.

Of course, you can also take advantage of the years you've spent building up your personal credit by using it to buy or rent the equipment you need to start your business. Leasing a computer or a vehicle means that more cash will be freed up for the day-to-day expenses of running your business, and it can buy you the time you'll need to establish your business. After all, not every customer will pick up the phone the first time they hear about your business; you'll need the extra time to win over the reluctant customer who wants to make sure you'll be around in six months to complete his project. If you choose this route, try to insert the name of your business into the lease documents. That way, even though the rental agreement is listed under your name, if you also include the name of your business it's a step towards establishing credit in the name of your business only. It can be difficult to get a corporate credit card or business lease when you are first starting out; establishing a business checking account is easy, however, and will provide future creditors with financial records of your business from day one.

Another way to personally finance your business is to take advantage of the assets you've already accumulated, but without depleting them. This, of course, is accomplished by using your personal credit cards or by taking out a home equity loan or a second mortgage to cover start-up costs and to buy business equipment.

A surprisingly large number of entrepreneurs raise at least part of the capital for start-up and operating expenses by asking friends and family and previous business colleagues to lend a monetary hand. Though some may ask for partial ownership in your fledgling firm, most will be satisfied by your personal guarantee of a payback date— usually with interest. Though you may be the most enthusiastic person in the world when it comes to

One mail-order publishing entrepreneur reports that after she installed an 800 phone line and began accepting credit cards for payment, her business doubled in just the first month. Other mail-order businesses report similar results. The increase in volume more than pays for commissions (typically 1–5 percent of the purchase price) paid to the bank.

your business, many people will want to know about your own financial commitment before they invest anything. To some it may not matter; but most people will want to know that you're willing to risk some of your own assets before they will provide your business with the capital you desperately need.

Though you might like to believe that banks and other financial institutions are just waiting for you to show up and give your five-minute spiel before they cheerfully write you a check for whatever amount you need to start your new business, the truth is that given their federal ties and restrictions, they will probably be reluctant to loan a start-up business money until a decent track record and a viable business has been established. Even then, they may require a significant chunk of collateral or set stringent contract terms to safeguard their investment.

Banks are more likely to give you a personal loan even though you will use it for business purposes. It definitely helps if you already have an established relationship with a bank for your personal accounts; you may want to ask for a small loan in the name of your business that you can pay back in one year. Once you have established a record of prompt payments with your business, the bank may be more likely to loan you larger amounts or provide you with a line of credit that you can draw against as needed.

The Small Business Administration also has numerous guaranteed loan programs available to small businesses, even start-ups, but they tend to be associated with banks, so you still have to apply for these loans through banks.

Of course, depending upon your business, arranging for customers to pay up front—while providing a small discount—will help improve the cash flow of any business. You'll need to gauge your business, customers, and how much money you are likely to generate from this technique, and if it's worth it to provide the discount. In many cases, it is.

Venture capitalists and other equity investors are in the headlines for their help in growing high-tech or other companies 1,000 percent or more each year. But for the great majority of small companies who do not expect to gross more than a hundred thousand dollars in the first year, venture capital is another galaxy. Venture capital and private angel investors look for fast growth, and incredible returns on their money in a short period of time. The bad news is that these investors typically request a sizable ownership chunk—25 to 50 percent usually—and somewhere down the road, if they don't agree with the way you're growing your company, they won't hesitate to unceremoniously boot you out.

As a rule, the acceptance rate for businesses they agree to fund is ridiculously low: they get bombarded with thousands of business plans, but they usually invest in a few can't-lose companies. Most entrepreneurs will never need a venture capitalist.

How much are you willing to risk in order to start your business? If you're like many Americans, you're probably long on debt and possessions but short on savings. If your heart skipped a beat when you first saw the total amount you think you need to start your business, there are options. Some are more drastic than others, but remember: Running a business is a risky venture in most parts. You'll have to take risks every day in the course of doing business. You might as well get used to it now.

Extending Credit to Customers

If you plan to start a business where it's standard procedure to collect payment before you provide your product or service to customers, you can skip this section. Obviously, most retail businesses conduct pay-as-you-go transactions: customers can choose to not use their own money to pay up front by using a credit card; however, their purchase then becomes more expensive with the subsequent interest charges if they don't pay it off all at once. But that's their problem, not yours. You still get paid up front.

If yours is a service-oriented business, or some other type of enterprise for which it is the industry standard for customers to pay for services rendered after you complete the work, possibly long after they receive it, well, that's another story. The debt-collection industry is growing by leaps and bounds, and not just by negotiating with consumers to pay a long-ignored credit card bill, either. Business owners who may have hired your company to perform services were most likely fully confident that they would be able to pay your bill when it came due thirty days down the road. Sometimes life takes unexpected twists, however, which means you may have to chase them all the way to small claims court, or perhaps hire an attorney who specializes in collections to do your dirty work.

Most business owners with overdue accounts do not get to this stage deliberately. Once you start your business, you'll discover how unexpected turns and twists in the entrepreneurial road can quickly turn your dreams of great success into scrambling to keep the light bill paid. This is how you may become low priority on a customer's accounts payable list.

Again, it depends on the type of business you run, but where net thirty is the rule, try to collect 50 percent of the total fee before you commence working when you undertake any new customers. Then you can bill once again after you complete the project.

Better yet is to arrange to bill a client's credit card in installments. That way, you're more likely to be paid in full. The time frame you'll receive your money in—sooner, rather than later or maybe not at all—is worth the few percentage points you'll pay the credit card company for having the privilege of merchant status. In fact, since many Americans use plastic for almost everything imaginable—and the majority pay their bills in full each month—it's worth your while to become qualified to accept MasterCard, Visa, and American Express. The more choices you provide your customers, the easier it will be for them to pay you, and the more likely they will choose you over a competitor who doesn't make it as easy for them to pay when their cash is a little low.

Now That You Can Show Us the Money

Though many aspiring entrepreneurs make money the major sticking point between thinking about starting a business and then going out and actually doing it, you'll see that a little bit of knowledge can go a long way toward demystifying the dollars-and-cents side of operating your own company.

Then again, the same could be said of the attitude that many people have toward technology. So hold tight and continue on: by the time you've finished reading chapter 6, you'll understand better how computers work and how they can act as your right-hand man in helping you manage your business.

THE BOTTOM LINE

For years, you may have convinced yourself that you're not good at math. When it comes to running your business, if you can understand the difference between a cash flow statement and a balance sheet, believe me: you're good at math, at least the kind of math that counts when it comes to your success as an entrepreneur.

Besides, when it is your money tied up in your company, you will want to learn as much as you possibly can about more advanced terms like *deviation analysis* and *funds flow from operations*. Use the information in this chapter as your springboard.

Technologically Speaking

I f you were starting a business ten years ago, you could have probably managed with no more technology than a telephone. Since you are starting your business today, it is pretty much a given that you will need a computer, voice mail system, and fax to help you run your business, at the very least. Entrepreneurs who used to put off buying a faster computer or a new software program because they didn't have the time to even think about learning them no longer have that excuse since, in most cases, even the most sophisticated software programs today have a pretty short learning curve.

The technological advances that took hold in the eighties and nineties have resulted in computers and software that make it so easy to run a business that you often have much more time to do the things you like to do best because the computer is taking care of the grunt work for you. Now that you can dictate all kinds of documents into your computer using voice-recognition programs, administrative assistants and other clerical employees are freed up to perform other tasks for you—unless, that is, they decide to quit and start their own businesses.

Computers

Once upon a time, when it came to your primary computer system, you had two choices: state of the art or what you could manage to buy at an affordable price.

Today, you can get both, along with as many special add-ons and features as you can cram onto a hard drive. But when it comes to basic computer systems, the technological advances and rapid change is dizzying: In 1996, having one gigabyte of storage space on your hard drive seemed like overkill to most people. Two years later, four gigs quickly became the standard-bearer, at one-quarter of the price of its two-year-old—ancient by high-tech standards—predecessor.

With powerful computer systems readily available and extremely affordable, there is no excuse to not buy a system that has as much power as you can afford, which is probably a lot more than you need.

Which Platform?

The first decision you'll have to make is whether you want a personal computer (PC) or a Macintosh. For some people, the choice is political, for others it's practical, though the gap is narrowing every day when it comes to the difference between the two platforms. People used to be concerned with the ability to transfer files from one platform to another, for example from a PC to a Mac or vice versa; now it's an issue of being able to find software for the Mac, since many software manufacturers no longer feel it's worth the expense to produce programs for what they feel is a minority segment of computer users.

Do You Need Portability?

The next decision you will need to make involves portability. Do you want your computer to be located primarily in your office, or do you think you will need to take it with you? Some entrepreneurs want to have both, while others only need a desktop. Technology is one of those funny things, where you do not know that you need something until you give it a try. Then once you get used to it, you wonder how you ever lived without it. Though laptops typically do not have the hard-drive storage capacity of desktop computers, the truth is that the majority of businesspeople do not need massive hard drives. You can always attach modules for zip drives, CD drives, and even an external hard drive to take care of any storage overflow. An advantage laptops have is that if you spend time out of the office taking notes on a regular basis, entering data directly onto a laptop saves you from having to enter it again, as you would if you took notes by hand first. Plus, if you need to demonstrate something to a customer or pull up some figures, the file is right there, which saves you from having to get back to the client later, when he or she may have changed his or her mind. And if you need to check out some facts on the Internet, again, you can do it on the spot.

Some people invest the majority of their computer budget in a laptop, and then get a less powerful and much less expensive desktop model for their office. This approach allows you to have the best of both worlds.

Vendors

In either case, it's a good idea to go with a well-known computer brand that offers a decent warranty. Or, you can visit a computer reseller in your area, usually a small shop that builds computers to your specifications and provides service after the sale. Many entrepreneurs find that they prefer this route, particularly if the company proves to be available to answer your questions in a relatively quick fashion and also provides a warranty for all purchases. After all, your time is too valuable to waste and will be in increasingly short supply once your business is up and running; you don't want to waste time on the phone waiting for a technical support representative to help you with a hard-drive problem.

Since computer standards and the technology change so rapidly, you will need to do your own research when it comes to figuring out how much RAM will be ideal for your computer, as well as other hardware specifications. Not only are everyone's needs different, but by the time you read this, anything that's currently state of the art will probably be obsolete. So do your homework and take advantage of the things you learn. It will help you run your business more efficiently and effectively.

Other Hardware

One of the most frequently made predictions at the dawn of the personal computer era turned out to be dead wrong. "The office of the future will be paperless," proclaimed the experts. If the office at your small business turns out like most, you'll probably be buried in the stuff.

Who knows how this happened? Hindsight won't reduce the number of documents you print out, but it's highly likely that after your computer, your printer will turn out to be the most important piece of hardware you'll buy for your small business. It's important to get the right one for your needs. Here's what to look for.

SMART SOURCES

Worried about how easy it is for computer thieves to steal your laptop when you're out and about, possibly losing all the hard work that you didn't have time to save on backup disks or drives?

CyberAngel, from Sentry, lies dormant in your laptop—until some unscrupulous sort makes off with it. When the thief tries to access your files without the correct password, the computer will lock up. And if the perpetrator plugs it in to try to use the modem, hoping that a well-placed phone zap will unlock it, CyberAngel will automatically contact Sentry headquarters, providing information on the exact location of the laptop. Sentry will then call you with the coordinates, providing you with enough info to call the cops.

CyberAngel
www.sentryinc.com

Ink Jet Printers

For the majority of the printing jobs you'll do in your business, an ink jet printer is probably your best choice. Ink jets outsell lasers for two reasons: they print in color as well as in black and white, and their text print quality is so crisp that it's virtually indistinguishable from laser printer output.

When selecting a printer, you should pay particular attention to the print quality, which traditionally is measured in dots per inch *(dpi)*, and is also referred to as resolution. Most ink jets print from 300 to 720 *dpi* vertically and horizontally, with some that use special modes requiring two passes through the printer—and therefore more time—to print at 1,200 or even 1,440 *dpi*.

However, *dpi* is not the only measure of quality you should look for in an ink jet printer. The speed of your printer, described as pages per minute *(ppm)*, is also an important consideration. Ink jets have traditionally printed at a slower rate than lasers—two to four pages per minute as compared to the four to six *ppm* capability of a laser—but ink jets are rapidly gaining ground.

The first ink jet printers that hit the market required specially treated paper to avoid fuzzy images, but thankfully that's no longer the case. Plain paper works well for most documents and images, although for important documents and photographs, you will want to invest in special bright-white ink jet papers and other photographic quality papers.

Laser Printers

If you're 100 percent sure you won't need to use color in the documents you print in the office, then you should spring for a laser printer. Besides being faster, documents produced by a laser printer contain darker, sharper text; it's no wonder that "laser quality" is still the primary standard by which all output from other printers is judged.

Laser printers print around four to twenty-four pages per minute, regardless of the amount of text or density of the images on the page, unlike an ink jet printer, which tends to get bogged down with an increase in text complexity and images. With laser printers, however, the amount of time it takes to print the first page is usually at least twice as long as for each subsequent pages, because of the time it takes for the computer to process and then send the digital image to the printer. To speed things up you should look for a printer that claims to have a fast first-page printing time.

Plain paper works fine for most laser printer jobs, but as is the case with an ink jet printer, for special jobs you may want to invest in higher quality stock. Laser printers have the advantage of being able to print directly on labels, transparencies, card stock, and envelopes.

Scanners

Scanners allow you to run an image or a document directly into a computer file, where you can then edit the text and manipulate the graphic. Like printers, they work on a *dots per inch* standard, and allow you to scan the image in order to catch a minimum of detail or as rich a representation as you'd like.

Like printers, scanners have also experienced great technological advances. There are handheld scanners as well as flatbeds that work in much the same way as a copy machine does, but while the handheld models were once more affordable than flatbeds—but less accurate—today the flatbeds are your best bet in the office. A portable handheld model is best if you need to scan items when you are out of the office.

You'll need special software in order to scan an image and then process it, but most of what you'll need comes already bundled when you buy the scanner.

Multifunction Peripherals

If you want a printer to be more than just a printer, you should spring for a multifunction unit that not only prints, but also sends and receives faxes, copies, scans, and can also serve as a voice-mail center.

Multifunction peripherals utilize ink jet technology to carry out their various tasks. They're appealing to business owners who don't want to clutter up a small office with four or more different pieces of electronic equipment when one would do it all, and do a good job at that.

When multifunction devices first came out, they could only print in one color, but their ink jet roots now provide them with the capability of all the colors of the rainbow. More so than with the other machines, multifunction peripherals rely on sturdy paper-handling ability, since they will be used in a variety of ways. You should look

Pets and Office Equipment

One of the best things about running your own business is that you get to choose with whom you're going to work. For some people, that means a cat or dog. Your equipment may not be as happy about your furry companions, however, due to stray fur, wagging tails, or an Olympic-caliber jumping ability.

There are precautions you can take to protect your electronic equipment from animal by-products. First, you should clean all equipment twice as often as you would if there were no animals by your side. Gather all loose wires and bundle them together to keep them from becoming chew toys; a spray called Bitter Apple, available in pet stores, will help protect them even more.

Two of the most inconvenient things that can happen with a cat or dog are a phone suddenly disconnected by an ill-placed paw, or a garbled message on your monitor composed during the three seconds you turned your back. Take it in stride, and take regular petting breaks because the short attention span of office pets is great for helping to prevent carpal tunnel syndrome in their human owners.

for a sturdy paper-feed tray for originals, an ample tray for paper stock (one hundred sheets or more), and a good-size output tray. And in case you run out of paper or ink when you're out of the office, the ability to receive and store twenty or more pages in memory is crucial.

Overall, multifunction peripherals are great if you don't have the space for separate units, especially if you don't use any one of the functions with great frequency. Otherwise, you should spring for a stand-alone machine that can handle heavy-duty jobs.

Choosing Software: What You Need to Do

Though the majority of computers today come loaded with more kinds of software than you'll probably ever use, it's likely you'll need at least one kind of software that is specific to your industry.

Much of the software you'll need to perform the simplest business tasks—from writing letters to keeping track of your customer list—comes packaged together so you only have to load one piece of software in order to get three or more programs onto your hard drive. Of course, you still have to load a number of floppy disks—or at least the contents of one CD—but the advantage of these bundled packages is that the programs are designed to work seamlessly with each other, making the transfer of the contents of a word processing file into a database program easy. Plus, it's cheaper to buy them all together than separately.

Many software manufacturers allow you to try out their programs before you purchase, by letting you download a scaled-down version or a full-fledged version that turns into a pumpkin after a limited period of time or number of uses. So if you're unsure whether a particular program will help your business to grow, see if you can try it for free first.

Here's a rundown of the different kinds of software you'll most likely need to run your business.

Word Processing

A word processing program allows you to input and then manipulate words to create documents like letters, reports, even booklets. One of the

greatest time-savers of word processing programs is the ability to merge fields from a database into a document, saving you from having to change the name, address, and salutation in each letter.
Leading brands: Microsoft Word, WordPerfect

Spreadsheets

Spreadsheets are a kind of graphical calculator, where it's possible to create financial charts of your revenue and expenses or inventory, and keep track of as many different values as possible. These are great for making budget forecasts, because they allow you to see how changing the amount in one category automatically alters all your other figures.
Leading brands: Excel, Claris

Accounting

Financial software allows your checkbook to come alive, integrating account information from inventory lists, price lists, invoices, customer files, and other bookkeeping information. Most programs will even print out your checks for you; all you have to do is sign them.
Leading brands: QuickBooks, Quicken, MS Money

Database

Database software is similar to spreadsheet programs, except instead of processing numbers it processes names and other information. You can sort your customer list alphabetically, by zip code, or by any other criteria you specify.
Leading brands: Access, Goldmine

F.Y.I.

Because entrepreneurs are getting so much of their research and buying and selling done via the web and e-mail, the potential for catching a computer virus is higher than ever. It's vital to have an antivirus software program that will check your hard drive for viruses when you first turn on your computer and again, when you log off. Norton AntiVirus is perhaps the best-known antivirus software (www.symantec.com); some others are McAfee VirusScan (www.networkasso-ciate.com) and IBM AntiVirus (www.ibm.com).

Desktop Publishing

Once upon a time, business owners had to hire expensive graphic artists to paste up art and copy for brochures, newsletters, and other promotional materials. The publishing software available today makes it possible for anyone to create materials that look like they came from a professional designer. It's no wonder, since the templates in these programs that make creating brochures as easy as cutting and pasting electronically were designed by crackerjack graphic artists.

Leading brands: Quark, Publisher

Graphics

You can create a pen-and-ink drawing, change the color of any image, or airbrush a photograph with graphics programs. One click and your mouse becomes a calligraphy pen, a paintbrush, pencil, or whatever else you'd like to use.

Leading brands: Illustrator, PaintShop

Telecommunications

If you want to send a fax via computer, visit the web, or send e-mail, you'll need to install software that can handle it. Most often, your gateway to the Internet—an Internet service provider or one of the big guys like America Online—will provide you with the software you need. If you're not on AOL, in order to read and send e-mail, you'll need to get your own software, which you can download for free, and software that will let you browse the Internet, also free for the downloading.

Voice Recognition

When it comes to the one technological development that most resembles the lifestyle of the Jetsons, voice recognition software has got to be it. Essentially, this software allows you to talk to your computer and have the words appear on your monitor as you speak. You can then transfer your words into any kind of software, most commonly word processing programs. You can also give the voice recognition software directions such as Print or Stop, and your wish is its command. Two good programs include ViaVoice and Naturally Speaking, and they come with everything you need to get started for under $100.

Shopping for Software

When shopping for software, take your time. You will need to compare the different features of programs that appear to be identical at first glance.

One way that many people—even experienced computer users—make mistakes is by not reading the System Requirements on the software box before they buy. In other words, you may discover that the software that proposes to do everything you need plus more, is simply not right for your computer. It may need more RAM than you have, consume more space on your hard drive than you would like, or require a later version of Windows.

Of course, many of these issues can be remedied, but not without additional cost. And if you've been meaning to upgrade your computer—or buy an entirely new system—buying the wrong program may be just the excuse you've been looking

SMART SOURCES

Two independent consumer-complaint sites to investigate information on computer software and hardware are the following:

www.gripenet.com

www.buyerpower.com.

Most people know that when you buy a new mouse or modem, you'll need to install the software that comes with it. What people don't know is that you'll first need to uninstall the software for your old mouse, or else chaos will result. To uninstall, use Norton's Uninstall program or refer to the manual that came with the mouse or modem you're uninstalling.

for. But it still pays to read the fine print first, because if you should decide to return the software to the store, the retailer may only allow you to trade the program for one that's identical to it—and it still won't work in your machine; other retailers will charge a restocking fee of between 10 percent and 25 percent of the price you paid for the program.

Check for Support

Another software feature you'll want to pay close attention to before you buy is how you can contact the company if you need technical support. Indeed, a number of entrepreneurs will refuse to buy a program with more features than a program that's less well endowed if it's rumored that the company with the better product makes it difficult for its customers to reach tech support in a timely fashion. As an entrepreneur, poor support is unacceptable if your relationship with a particular client may hang in the balance.

One way to check a company out is to head to the web. Find a Usenet group, industry forum, or an Internet mailing list to find others who have used the program and have had experience with the company's technical support department.

Register

The first thing you must do when you bring a new software program home, before you even install it, is to fill out the registration card. Or do it while you're installing the program, and automatically e-mail your information to the manufacturer. This way, when—not if—you have a problem, the technician you call at the company will be able to help you because his records show that you actually purchased the program, and are not using a copy. If it is an unpurchased copy, he'll probably hang up.

Check the Web

When a problem does come up, you—a registered user—should head for the company web site for information on tech support. Check the FAQ (list of frequently asked questions that help you to troubleshoot the problem on your own before calling for help) or the company's faxback services. If these don't help you to diagnose and fix the problem, it's a good idea to take the double-barreled approach: send an e-mail to the technical support department as well as to the customer service department. Describe the problem you're having and include the things you've already done to try to remedy the situation.

If you're particularly desperate, call for tech support, although the amount of time you may have to spend waiting on hold is longer than the time it will take a technical support representative to e-mail an answer back to you.

To Network, or Not to Network?

After people became comfortable working with, and then utterly dependent on, computers in their

SMART MONEY

Small-business owners who are just starting out often lack the funds to invest in a full-fledged network server and software but would benefit from using one.

Gregg Ramsay, Ph.D., a network consultant and technology coordinator at Kimball Union Academy, a private school in Meriden, New Hampshire, has a simple solution. In fact, you can probably start networking immediately. Just use your e-mail accounts to share files, documents, even web links with other employees and independent contractors, whether they work in your office or off site. If you're using the same programs, so much the better, but even e-mailing a document in the body of an e-mail will enable the recipient to cut and paste the material into another program.

SMART DEFINITION

Dial-Up Networking (or DUN)

DUN combines a computer network with the mobility of portable computers. DUN allows employees and designated people to connect with a company's server and network by using a modem and standard telephone lines, no matter where the people are calling from. If you plan to use off-site employees and independent contractors in your business, consider upgrading your network to include access from the outside.

jobs, the next issue to arise concerned how they could share a file or other information with coworkers. The early solution was to pass disks back and forth. Given the rapid developments in technology, people thought there had to be a better way. At the same time, business owners got tired of buying a printer for every computer in the office. Why couldn't they just be linked together?

The best answer arrived in the form of a computer network. If you plan to have at least one other person working with you in your business, you should seriously consider installing a computer network to streamline your work. Most people within an office occasionally need to share something, whether it's data, programs, printers, or hard drives. If the data you wish to share is not sensitive in nature, and if the need to share occurs frequently enough, a small office network would be easier than swapping disks or desks.

The desire to share a printer is frequently the first spark that starts a small business on the road to a network. After all, why equip three to ten computers with their own printers when, depending on the physical size and location of the office, you can set up a small network and share one or two printers within close proximity to the computers?

Private versus Shared Data

Before you decide whether or not to network your small business, you must first take a hard look at your data. All of your data should be classified as either sensitive or nonsensitive. Sensitive data is information that might cause harm to either the company or to employees of the company if the information was leaked or otherwise divulged to prying eyes. One example of sensitive data is payroll and accounts payable information. If your competition is aware of your accounts payable balances and history, they may undercut your prices or offer better terms to your customers. Or, if an employee knows what you are paying your other employees, he or she can use that information to bargain for a pay raise. Employee appraisals are also among the most sensitive data that can be stored on a small business's computers, so it's a good idea to place this data on a private computer that's not on the company-wide network or on floppy disks, zip drives, or tapes that can be stored in a fireproof box.

Nonsensitive data is any information that is commonly and publicly available, or that can be easily obtained through methods other than hacking or breaking into the computer's database system. Your sales price list would be considered to be nonsensitive data.

F.Y.I.

Blindly paying your phone bill each month could be costly—you unknowingly may be paying for extra services.

Also, another overlooked expense when starting a new business is connecting a fax machine to a toll-free number. This can add unnecessary charges for a service that isn't significantly resulting in more business or profits.

Do You Need a Server?

Once you've decided to install a network for your business, you need to determine which type of network is best. Though there are many different types of networks available, there are two worth noting for the small business just starting out: a server-less network and a server-based network. Both are relatively simple to maintain, diagnose the problems of, and to set up.

In a **server-less network**, each computer is connected to the others in a line using coaxial cable. Besides the cable, you'll need a network card and a network-based software program—like Windows NT—and that's it. Each computer or user in the network is given a unique name and password in order to access the other hard drives that are linked together via the network. In a server-less network, no one computer controls the network, and all shared resources are controlled by individual computers.

A **server-based network** differs in that one computer—referred to as the server—in the link controls the entire network. Most often, a server-based network has two functions: A file server contains data that all networked users can access, while a print server acts as a queue to organize print jobs before they are sent on to the printer. In this configuration, the server hosts all or most of the shared data or information; users must log directly on to the server to access the necessary data. A password and user name are still required to access a server-based network. If your company's employees don't want others to start nosing around their own hard drives, then you should choose a server-based network over a server-less network.

Hooking up a server-based network is more complex than installing a server-less network, but any computer-savvy individual can do it with one of the comprehensive networking books on the market; the advice of a computer expert at a local shop who can also provide him with all of the network cards, cables, and software he needs; and lots of patience.

Telephone Systems

You probably think that it's easy to select the right phone system for your business. Because even if you do most of your business over the phone with customers, your present system will work just fine, and as long as you answer your phone with your business name between the hours of nine and five, you're fine. Right?

Try again. If you just want to receive and place phone calls—and nothing else—a single-line phone will work well. However, things are seldom that simple, even for a person who's working by himself in a modest home office.

Even if you are working alone, you should get an additional phone line to use solely for business. Then use your home number—which probably isn't used much by other family members during the day—as your combination fax/Internet access line and the business line as your primary form of communication. Or else you can use the business line for incoming calls and the residential line for outgoing, since in most cases in-state toll calls are more expensive for a business than for a personal number.

Voice Mail Options

For voice mail capabilities, you can use the services offered by your local phone company, buy a software system for your computer, or get a stand-alone unit with a receiver. The computer-based software applications have multiple functions, including the ability to fax. And more advanced programs offer multiple mailboxes, paging, and call forwarding choices. You can even tie incoming numbers into your database program so that when a customer calls, your computer will instantly take note and his database information will appear on the screen before the second ring.

The downside to these more complex programs

WHAT MATTERS, WHAT DOESN'T

What Matters
• You can travel light with a cell phone that offers a digital phone, tiny computer monitor, and keyboard with e-mail capabilities.

• Batteries! If you have a laptop, make sure you carry extras with you and that they're fully charged.

• A beeper allows you to be accessible, but not *too* accessible.

What Doesn't
• A phone glued to an ear every waking moment. No one is so important.

• Using a voice mail system designed for a major corporation if your operation is a small business.

• Announcing to the world that you've "got to check your messages."

is that they're not only more expensive and difficult to setup, but in order for them to operate, your computer must be turned on twenty-four hours a day. Stand-alone units work well, but are often limited in the services they offer. So are voice mail services offered by the phone company, but they have one big advantage, they can still accept and process calls even if you have lost power—which is a special problem for entrepreneurs who live in areas where power surges and outages are common, and can render stand-alone units and computer-based voice mail software totally useless.

More Power

If you have at least a few other people working in your office, you'll need something more powerful to transfer calls from one line to another. You'll also need multiple mailboxes, not only for each employee but for other options, including taking customer names, placing orders, and leaving general messages. A simple but costly solution is Centrex service, which is available from your local phone company. With Centrex you'll have multiple phone lines and voice mail at one site with the potential to add several other locations in the same state to create a single seamless statewide phone system.

A precursor to Centrex which is still used widely is a phone switch, also known as a PBX, or private branch exchange. PBX tends to be cheaper than Centrex, but requires more maintenance and ongoing work to keep it up and running. A third option, and probably the most reasonable if you're just starting out but need a multiple-user phone line, is a hybrid system available from most phone network vendors that specialize in business solutions. These hybrid systems offer analog or digital multi-line phones along with voice mail. Many manufacturers offer hybrids, so it's easy to get the services you need at a reasonable price, along with responsive maintenance and troubleshooting.

Fax Machines

With fax machines, the choice of whether to use traditional thermal paper or plain paper is up to you. However, if you want to project a professional image for your business from the start, you'll need a dedicated fax line, or at least one that is hooked up to a call splitter that can distinguish between incoming faxes and regular phone calls. As discussed earlier, you may want to investigate the multifunction devices that incorporate fax, copying and scanning capabilities. Just make sure that callers will be able to reach it directly, and don't have to call you first to tell you to turn it on. Not only is this unprofessional, but it sends the wrong message to customers.

If you want to reap the revenue that other entrepreneurs do and you do a lot of business over the phone, you must first act like a real business. Otherwise, your customers and suppliers are not going to treat you like a real business. Even if you are the sole employee of You, Inc., you'll need to rethink your phone approach, though that doesn't mean you'll have to spring for a complex multiline phone system, either.

The great thing about doing most of your business by phone is that you can project a professional demeanor to your clients but be as comfortable as you want, whether that means working in your pajamas or outside in a hammock.

What's Next?

Okay, so now you know what you need to bring your business up-to-date technologically speaking, from computers to phone systems. In order to make those phones and faxes ring off the hook, you first have to let the world know you exist.

You will do this by marketing your business. And you will learn how in the next chapter.

THE BOTTOM LINE

The high-tech revolution that first got our collective attention in the early 1980s started in the business world, where business owners and employees were eager to incorporate new technology in order to make it easier to get their work done.

Today, new developments are still appearing in business, still in an effort to accomplish more work in less time and with less expense. Use as much technology as you can afford; proceed without it, and you may always wonder what you would have been able to accomplish.

Marketing Your Business

Marketing is the art of letting people know about your business in as many ways as possible. The marketing methods you choose—advertising, publicity, or a Web page—depend on the type of business you're running, your budget, how quickly you want to grow your business, and the size of the audience you're trying to reach and where they're located. Regardless of the kind of marketing you do, it's important to keep in mind that it needs to be consistent. It can also be fun and the most creative part of a business.

The Purpose of Marketing

A business may have the biggest, best, fastest, or cheapest product or service in the world, but unless people know about it, there's no point to starting it in the first place.

The purpose of marketing is to plan and carry out a variety of strategies that will first inspire new customers to give you a try. Then once they have become your customers, it's necessary to market to them so they return.

When you first start your business, every customer is a new customer. Therefore, the types of marketing that you use to let the world know about your business should focus on getting new customers to walk through the door or pick up the phone to call you. Once a business has been up and running for a while, the way that you market it—as well as the methods you use—will change.

In time, marketing to repeat customers should

become the focus of most of your marketing efforts for the simple reason that repeat customers are the lifeblood of any business. In fact, one often-quoted statistic says that 80 percent of a company's business comes from 20 percent of its customers. And the good news about marketing to repeat customers is that getting them to come back is usually less expensive than getting a new customer to try out a business in the first place, since most people need to receive several exposures to a company's message before they decide to check it out. It's not necessary to sell your current customers on the benefits they'll derive from your business, since they're already familiar with them.

Two Kinds of Marketing

Marketing is an essential part of every business. Basically, there are two primary forms of marketing: external and internal.

External marketing primarily involves methods that are used to acquire new customers, but they can also serve to reinforce your business in the minds of current customers. External marketing techniques include:

• Advertising in newspapers and magazines and on radio and TV

• Being quoted in articles and news stories

• Sending informational brochures through the mail, and designing and promoting a Web page

Entrepreneurs frequently disagree on whether to put more effort into external or internal marketing: one requires more money while the other requires more time, both of which tend to be in short supply when starting a business.

Jim Trounson, founder and president of Medical Management in Boise, Idaho, a firm that provides office management for physicians, believes entrepreneurs should spend more time than money on marketing, not only when first starting a business but also later, after establishing a strong customer base. "A better-managed business ends up being its own marketer," he says. "When a patient walks into one of our clinics, it will be a pleasant, productive experience, which will bring him back again and again."

Internal marketing involves the message a business conveys once it has direct contact with customers and can influence their buying decisions. Internal marketing can be subtle, as in the grooming and appearance of staff members, or more direct, as in sending a note thanking a customer for her business.

External marketing tends to be easier to plan for and to measure the results, but it can be more expensive than internal marketing. On the other hand, internal marketing can be harder to plan and institute, but in the long run it can be more effective in building repeat customers than external marketing.

Sending a Message

Regardless of whether you choose to focus on one type of marketing in the beginning—or both—it's important to send a clear message describing how your product or service will help to make your customers' lives better or easier.

One mistake that entrepreneurs often make is to write advertisements and press releases that are focused on their business, and not on their customers. For instance, a computer store may send out a press release announcing the addition of an assistant manager. A potential customer may read this in the paper, say, "So what?" and turn the page.

Instead, the company should tell customers how this new development will help make their lives easier. For example, does this new staff addition mean that customers can visit the store until nine every night instead of six? Can the store's service staff now make house calls? If this is the case, then you should say so, and convey this information in every single piece of information you use to promote your business.

Today, if you want to immediately grab someone's attention, one of the most important benefits you can stress is how your product or service can save a customer time. While some entrepreneurs will want to tell customers how they can save money, time and again public opinion polls report that many people say that saving time is more important to them than saving money.

To ensure consistency, an entrepreneur should make sure that the message being sent to customers is the same in all marketing materials. Although more established businesses tend to use a variety of themes to market to different audiences, beginning entrepreneurs have enough on their plates. Keep things simple by picking one market to target as well as one message to concentrate on from the beginning.

Distinguish Yourself from the Competition

Another way to develop your message is to establish what sets your business apart from the competition. What does your business do differently from other businesses that are competing for the same market? The best way to answer this question is to view your business and your competitors' through the eyes of a prospective customer.

Say your lifelong dream is to start a gourmet food shop, but there are already three others serving the market you wish to reach. In order to dis-

SMART DEFINITION

Cooperative advertising

An arrangement between two or more businesses that share the cost of an ad, brochure, or other marketing tool to promote both businesses. Coop advertising is a marketing venture where a business includes the name of a product they sell in an ad, and the manufacturer of the product pays for a portion of the advertising cost. In many cases, coop advertising provides a small-business owner with a good way to increase the size and frequency of his ads without spending more than the marketing budget allows. For ideas, look at what your business offers customers and then hook up with a partner—a supplier or other complementary business—to help you reach more people at a lower cost.

tinguish your shop from all the others, you must first look at each with a critical eye: How are they different? More importantly, what is one service that consumers need but none of the shops are currently providing? In other words, you should look for a void in the marketplace to help distinguish your business from the competition.

Let's take a look: Whitmore's Gourmet Delight is open seven days a week while Deli Heaven specializes in New York–style delicatessen food. Bon Vivant focuses on shipping customized gift baskets around the world. Where's the void? What can you offer gourmet food lovers in your area that will make them want to visit your store and not the others?

Once you find a message that will help your business stand out, you should let your customers hear it, loud and clear. Any time you can say that your business is the only one around that provides a necessary service to customers, you'll set yourself apart and attract even more business.

Common Ways to Market Your Business

There are as many ways to market a business as there are types of businesses. With all the tasks that require an entrepreneur's time and attention when getting a new business off the ground, it's a good idea to pick a couple of marketing methods and concentrate on them.

Here are four of the most commonly used ways to market a business:

Advertising

Advertising is a type of marketing where a business pays for a certain amount of space in a magazine or newspaper, or airtime on radio or TV in order to tell its message to a particular kind of audience.

Most beginning entrepreneurs believe that they should focus most of their marketing attention on advertising. Not all advertising is the same, however, and depending on the message and on the audience, one form of advertising—radio, for example—might bring better results for a particular sale or event than another. Because advertising can be expensive, it's particularly important to plan ahead and ask pointed questions about what you can reasonably expect for a response if you decide to advertise.

Publicity

Getting the media to mention your business in a newspaper or magazine or on the radio can be one of the most effective ways to market your business. Except for the cost of preparing a press kit, postage, and phone calls, publicity costs you nothing but your time. In exchange, your business can receive stacks of press clips, lots of new business, and respect from customers as well as competitors. The best thing about publicity is that an appearance in the media is a tacit endorsement of your business by a respected outside source. After all, you didn't have to pay in order to be mentioned by the media, since the reporter or producer obviously thought enough of your business to let her audience know about it too.

SMART SOURCES

If you must buy one book on marketing, any one of Jay Levinson's titles from his *Guerrilla Marketing* series will provide you with more ideas than you'll know what to do with.

The premise behind guerrilla marketing is that small businesses must position and market themselves differently from the big guys by being on the offensive. The result is thousands of marketing techniques and ideas that are unique, and sometimes outrageous, but they succeed in getting the message out by talking loudly *and* carrying a big stick.

In marketing, remember that people everywhere are inundated by hundreds of media messages each day. Catching their eye is a real accomplishment. Be a guerrilla!

The standard way to contact the media is with a press kit, which essentially provides a good snapshot of your business. Here is what a press kit usually contains:

- Cover letter

- Press release

- A brochure

- Biographical information about you, your partner, or your employees

- Previous press clips, if available

- Glossy black-and-white photo

- A folder to hold it all

A press kit provides information about your business in a language that media people understand. Having a complete, informative press kit makes it more likely that a media person will do a story on your business, since a press kit provides many more pertinent details than do marketing materials that are aimed specifically at customers.

Direct Mail

Most people refer to this form of marketing as "junk mail," but the truth is that as life in America has become busier, noisier, and more complex, customers are more likely to respond to an offer they receive in the mail because they can review the information at their own convenience.

Direct Mail with an Impact!

In business, it's true: Appearances are everything! And your direct-mail package should not only be attractive, it should have everything your client or customer will need to do business with you. Here's what to do:

• **Write a letter.** It can be one page or eight, or more. Most average between two and four pages. Direct-mail experts say the longer the letter, the better the response.

• **Design an order form.** It should be easy for people to respond, whether by mail, fax, or phone. Look at other order forms you receive in the mail for ideas on how to format your own.

• **Include a reply envelope.** Needless to say, this should be smaller than the outside envelope. Some businesses arrange to pay for the return postage, others don't. Direct mail experts say that if a customer has to pay for the stamp to place an order, the likelihood that he'll respond will decrease.

• **Prepare an attractive outside envelope.** Include a teaser on the outside, as well as the name of your business and a return address. Experiment with different colors as well as a variety of teasers to see which ones bring the best response.

Direct mail marketing is most often used by companies that base all or part of their business on selling through the mail, though local service-oriented companies, like a landscaping business or beauty salon, can also market effectively with direct mail. The direct mail packages for these types of businesses probably won't contain many enclosures, perhaps only a coupon or postcard.

The secret to effective direct mail selling is to first select a mailing list that will bring a good response—either a list developed from a business's existing customer base or one rented from a mailing-list company—and then tinker with the contents of the direct mail package.

The Internet

Almost overnight, the Internet has become a vitally important way to market a business. Whether it is through creating a Web page, using automatic e-mail responses, or joining an Internet mailing list, you should be clear about your intentions—to provide information about your business, products, and services—and not expect overnight success just because you put your business online.

For many consumers and businesspeople, the Internet has become an easy way to perform initial research about a company before deciding to patronize it. After all, if a person is unfamiliar with a business, once he's checked out the Web site, odds are that he'll call the 800 number for a copy of the paper catalog and then place an order by using a more traditional form of communication: either by writing a check and sending it through the mail or by calling the toll-free number to use a credit card.

When the Internet first started to become widely used, businesses poured lots of money into developing fancy, entertaining Web pages, and then loudly complained when the number of orders received through the sites failed to pay for the production costs. So be savvy about your site, don't spend money needlessly, and remember it's the message that matters—not the slickness of the medium.

The Internet changes daily, and with those changes come more opportunities for savvy entrepreneurs to market their businesses. When it comes to brand-new marketing techniques that promise you the world, remember the old adage: if it sounds too good to be true, it probably is.

There are many other types of marketing—

including special events, trade shows, and tele-marketing—but the previous four present the best and most widely accepted ways to get your business off on the right foot.

Making a Plan

Entrepreneurs know to employ a variety of marketing techniques because it's impossible to predict how effective any one method will be until time and money has been spent. A marketing plan will help you to keep track of the various marketing methods and should be considered to be as essential to the success of your business as developing the business plan described in chapter 3.

Even though your customer base and business may change over time, a marketing plan should follow the goals that you want to reach during the first full year you're in business. A marketing plan can be fifty pages or longer, or just a few pages. Regardless of the length, a marketing plan should contain these primary components:

• **A description of your business's primary audience.** Who is the most likely market? Wholesale or retail customers? Men, women, or children? Local, regional, national, or worldwide?

• **A list of the marketing methods that will be used to reach this audience.** Keep in mind that there are countless ways to reach a single market. If your business caters to more than one market, your marketing plan will become more complex. Despite your focus, you should understand there will be some overlap, since no one lives in a vacuum. This

WHAT MATTERS, WHAT DOESN'T

What Matters:

• Asking your customers where they first heard of your business; otherwise, it's difficult to know if your marketing is working.

• Marketing is not selling. *Marketing* opens the door for a business, letting potential customers know it exists. *Selling* must be done the old-fashioned way: face to face.

• Taking the time to do one little thing to market your business each and every day.

What Doesn't:

• Spending lots of advertising dollars with one publication.

• Glitz, showing off, making promises that are impossible to keep. Simple is still best.

• Waiting around for "word of mouth" to take effect. You first have to get the word out so the mouths will know.

F.Y.I.

One common saying in the field of marketing goes like this: One line in the editorial section of a newspaper or magazine is worth at least ten lines of advertising. Entrepreneurs who are smart about marketing consider this formula when drawing up marketing plans in terms of time and budget.

is good news because the more times a prospective customer hears about your business, the more likely he is to remember it the next time he hears it, and the more likely he is to become a customer.

• **A schedule that lists the months in which the projects will begin and be completed.** To allow for long-range planning, creating a month-by-month list makes it easy to schedule marketing projects and to anticipate them. You may want to schedule more time-consuming projects for the months when business is expected to be slow—while you concentrate the easier and more expensive methods, like advertising, for the months where you have more money than time.

• **The person responsible for carrying out the project.** Entrepreneurs who are just starting out have enough on their plates without having to find time to stuff press kits into envelopes. But, while an MBA is not necessary to market a business, it is sometimes easier to get attention if the owner is the one calling reporters to check if they've received a press kit. It can also save the owner from having to train an employee. In your marketing plan, write the name of the person who will be responsible next to each project. And a week before the project is due to start, check with that person to see if everything is set to begin.

• **A budget for each project.** In many cases, these figures will have to be rough estimates. Doing the research ahead of time will help you to see if projected marketing costs—from postage to printing to advertising—are in line with your projected revenue. Average the marketing costs throughout the entire year and then compare the costs as a percentage of projected first-year revenues. In some months your marketing costs may run a lot higher than the overall percentage you've figured on, but as long as they stay in line for the year as a whole, you'll be on track.

Without a marketing plan, many business owners will only have hits and misses when it comes to their marketing. The great thing about having a marketing plan is that it can serve as a pretty reliable road map for the first year in the life of your business. Of course, it's necessary to tinker with it occasionally, but in most cases a quick glance at the plan once a week is enough to stay on track.

Who Is Your Customer?

Undoubtedly, the type of business you start will determine the people who will become customers. The first step to reaching customers is to draw up a profile of the kind of client you'd like to attract.

Defining your customer means you can then narrow down your choice of the marketing methods you use.

Your answers to the following questions will help you to define the ideal client or customer for your business.

SMART MONEY

Book-marketing expert John Kremer, author of *1001 Ways to Market Your Books*, says that to get full mileage from your marketing plan, you should make five new contacts every day to promote your business. "Whether it's calling an editor, sending out a press release to a new publication, or faxing a copy of an article to a distributor, these are all things that don't take long to do but the positive effect can really add up quickly when you do just five of them a day."

F.Y.I.

Contrary to popular opinion, the customer is not always right. There are some customers out there who are purposely nothing but trouble, while others will always want to get something for nothing. Smart business owners catch on after a couple of experiences reveal that certain people will never be satisfied no matter how much a company does for them. If you know you're providing a high-quality product or service and other customers are happy and keep coming back, take it as a clear sign to cut your losses and politely inform the troublesome customer that you choose not to do business with him any longer. Life is short: pursue the vast majority of customers who have had good experiences with your business.

Self-Assessment Quiz 5

1. When you close your eyes to imagine, who is the most likely type of customer that you can see walking through your door?

2. Where does this person live, and what kind of business does he or she work in?

3. What is your customer's income range?

4. What kind of shops does he or she frequent?

5. Which magazines does this person read?

6. Why will he or she become a customer in the first place?

7. What do you need to do to keep this customer coming back?

Let's say you want to start a day spa. The primary market for your business will probably consist of upper-middle-class women who are 25 to 55 years old. This information will help you to (a) determine the publications this market reads to help you decide where to advertise; (b) decide the months when you should advertise (spring fills some women with anxiety about the upcoming beach season); and (c) establish the particular services to promote in the ads, from waxing to anti-aging facials.

You should do as much research as possible in order to know your customers inside out, because every bit of information you gather about a potential market can then be used as a tool to find them.

It's also important to realize that no matter how much marketing you do, it's impossible for any one business to reach every person who is a prospective customer for its product or service. Think about it: your message is only one of thousands they see and hear every day. Consider what catches your eye in an ad or brochure, and then use these techniques to attract the customers who are best for your business.

Once your business is up and running and new customers are walking in your door every day, tap their expertise to further help you to define your overall customer base. Keep detailed records of each customer's individual preferences, and be sure to ask them how you can help them.

Your Marketing Budget

There is no right or wrong amount for a business to spend on marketing. Many factors will influence whether a business allots 5 percent of its total annual budget for marketing or 15 percent. Selecting a percentage for your business is the first step.

For new entrepreneurs, it can be difficult to accurately assess the practical difference between spending 5 percent or 15 percent on marketing because the figure is often affected by what is currently more in abundance: time or money. For instance, although 15 percent obviously buys a lot more ad space than 5 percent, inexpensive forms of marketing—like publicity and sponsoring community events—take more time than money, but can be much more effective.

Jim Hoskins had been working at IBM for ten years when he began to think seriously about starting his own business. Since he had authored several books on the side during his IBM tenure, he thought about starting a book publishing company.

Hoskins figured a surefire path to success would be to produce books that had a buyer already lined up. The first title at the company that would become Maximum Press was about a specialized software package developed by IBM. The corporation committed to purchase a certain number of books in advance. Hoskins made enough money from that first title to launch a line of computer books for consumers.

Moral of the story: Before starting a business, convince prospective customers to commit upfront to your product or service.

The next step is to figure how much of your marketing budget should go to each type of marketing by determining which marketing projects will be most effective to help establish the image of your business.

Here are some tips:

• Track the types of marketing your competitors use. Sign up for their mailing lists, see how often they change their Web sites, watch how often they advertise. Then use this information to plan and budget your own marketing program.

• If you plan to do business with a variety of markets, including retailers, wholesalers, and distributors, be sure to allocate a portion of your marketing budget to allow for the cost of promoting to these markets.

• If your budget is tight—and what entrepreneur's is not?—and your choice is between one thousand dollars of advertising or thousand dollars of direct mail, choose the latter. Though you'll probably reach fewer people, direct mail will not only generate more orders but also help you determine exactly where those orders are coming from. Advertising may boost the amount of traffic in your store or increase the number of phone inquiries, but it also requires more effort in the long run to convert those inquiries into sales. Advertising tends to build name recognition more than direct sales. Savvy entrepreneurs know before settling on a marketing tactic exactly what they wish to accomplish.

• One of the most difficult concepts for novice entrepreneurs to grasp is *not* that they have to spend money to make money. Rather, it's convincing them to loosen the pursestrings when business slows down. Especially when the economy slows, the first budget item that many businesses cut or eliminate entirely is marketing. This is the worst thing to do, for two reasons.

First, a business will receive less exposure to potential customers with a decrease in marketing, which then creates even less business, and so on. The second reason not to slash your marketing expenses, and an even more important one, is simply because your competitors are probably cutting theirs. For example, if you are one of five desktop publishing businesses in town, and four cut back on marketing while you increase yours, guess whose business will continue to grow despite the economy?

Be smart and consistent when drawing up a budget for marketing. It's possible to be frugal and still hit your target markets effectively.

You're Almost There

You're nearing the end of the *Smart Guide to Starting a Small Business.* You're probably chomping at the bit, figuring that you know everything necessary to get started in your business, but wait! Before you throw down the book and run out the door to start writing your business plan and forecasting your first year's revenue, take a look at the next chapter. "Putting It All Together" will alert you to the ways you should check in with your business after you've had your grand opening and are a few months down the road.

The best reason for reading it now is that later you'll be so busy growing your business that you may not have the time.

THE BOTTOM LINE

Think of marketing as a way to get closer to your customers while providing them with enough incentive to look forward to doing business with you. In the end, marketing is merely a communication tool. Whether you choose to use the equivalent of a megaphone or a whisper depends on your business, your budget, even your temperament.

Whatever you do, keep in mind that everything you do in the course of running your business is a form of marketing. View it as a chance to let the world know about the valuable service or product you provide.

CHAPTER 8

....

Putting It All Together

THE KEYS

• Regularly check in with the goals you set in your business plan to see if you need to alter your day-to-day strategy.

• Networking with people in your industry—and outside it—can be invaluable in making contacts who may turn into customers.

• Learning to effectively manage your time will help you to run your business more efficiently.

• Controlling the growth of your business means that you have more direction over its future.

• Starting a new business can be highly addictive; many entrepreneurs start a brand new company every few years.

You now have the knowledge and the tools that are necessary to start your own business. Congratulations!

As you know, you will be taking a new class in Entrepreneurship every single day that you are running your business. In fact, it may soon seem like you are getting paid not only to be your own boss, but also to learn the kinds of things you wished were taught in high school and college. Now, if you want to investigate something new for your business you can! And you don't have to get permission, either.

Each entrepreneur will learn more advanced business methods and practices in his own time, depending upon his temperament and the industry in which he's employed. Every new business owner, however, will face some of the following issues at one time in his entrepreneurial career. So take note.

Tracking Your Progress

How will you know if your business is growing not only at a pace you can handle but at a reasonable pace that will let you reach the goals you've set for yourself?

Easy. Check in with your business plan at least once or twice a month to see that you are on track with the goals and projects that you have set for the month, and to alert you to upcoming tasks for which you will have to prepare. Remember, you developed and selected each step of your business plan as a way to grow your business as each step is accomplished. So if one project is taking more time than you had planned, it may throw the rest of your growth timeline off kilter.

But that's not necessarily a bad thing. Keep in mind that you developed and wrote your business plan before you had a clue about the demands your business would place on you once you were up and running. The tendency to strive for a lot more than can be handled is a common occupational hazard of new entrepreneurs.

Watch the Numbers

That's why it's important to compare your sales figures and other benchmarks with the projections in your business plan. If you discover that you are consistently pulling in less revenue than you had projected, but are still able to cover your expenses, don't be too hard on yourself; you're obviously doing fine. Once you see that your early projections may have been overly optimistic, you may want to revamp some of the other projects you have scheduled for the rest of your first year in business. An abundance of enthusiasm is normal when you first start to plan your own business. However, now that you have a better idea of what it's really like and how much you're realistically able to accomplish in the course of one day, you should feel okay about adjusting your plans, since your business may have grown so quickly that you barely have time to take care of the customers you currently have, not to mention adding even more to your workload. After all, they haven't been able to clone humans . . . yet.

Who's Buying?

Another thing to watch for is where the majority of your sales are coming from. When you first started to plan your business, perhaps you thought you would tailor one service to four distinct groups of people. But now that you've been in business for several months, you find that more than half of your sales are derived from only one group.

There are several possible reasons for this. Perhaps it's the time of year in that particular industry when people are particularly alert to the product or service you offer, and so have noticed your ads and brochures more than your other targeted groups. Or it may be due to the fact that the people in this group are more closely knit than the others and word of mouth travels faster than lightning.

Or, face it, it could be that this group of customers were your best bet all along, something that you are only discovering after an initial period of trial and error. In any case, there are several things you can do. One is to continue marketing equally to all four groups, and hope that the other three just need more time to respond than the first. Or you can step up advertising campaign to the other three groups, figuring that perhaps they just need more of a nudge.

Or if you're getting as much business as you can handle from the group that's responding, you may want to either widen your reach of marketing to more people who fall under the same umbrella, or postpone future marketing to this market and steer the earmarked funds toward a totally new group of customers. In any case, as you learned in the last chapter, you need to continue marketing in order to keep your business in the minds of your current and prospective customers. When one group responds above and beyond the others, well, that's a good problem to have.

Networking

You often hear that it's not what you know, it's who you know. When it comes to running your own business, obviously both are important, but with all the tasks you have on your plate, you may find that getting together with other entrepreneurs—who are probably as consumed by their businesses as you are—is something that doesn't take priority in the course of your busy day.

This is a mistake. Joining a variety of business associations when you're first starting out can be absolutely invaluable in terms of the contacts you can make, as well as the advice you can get from more experienced entrepreneurs at no charge. The importance of networking for entrepreneurs— long considered to be lone wolves when it came to their businesses—first arose in the 1980s. The good news is that all kinds of trade and professional organizations are reporting wide increases in membership numbers; it means that businesspeople in all areas are discovering the value of networking. And that is great for you because it means you will have access to that many more experts and mentors who you can call on for advice.

In fact, many industry associations with local chapters often have informal programs where members can volunteer to provide a free hour of consultations to any other member. What a wonderful opportunity to pick the brain of a seasoned professional in your industry.

STREET SMARTS

Anyone can find unusual ways to network for contacts within his field or for new customers. Dr. Walter Funk spends his early mornings and early afternoons running a private practice in Strongsville, Ohio, and the rest of the time managing the Ace Hardware Store he bought in 1985, which is located less than a block from his office. His patients visit the hardware store, while his customers call on him when they require surgery, his medical specialty.

Do people in town think it is strange that the doctor they see in the morning might fix their screen door in the afternoon? "They were a little surprised at first, but it's worked out quite well, because I'd been in practice for thirty-one years. Besides," he says, "I call most of these people by their first names anyway." Networking at its best.

It's a good idea to join at least two different trade associations when you first start your business: make one an association that specializes in your chosen field, and the other a more general regional or statewide organization, like the Rotary, a local businesswomen's group, or chamber of commerce. And if one doesn't exist, then start your own by placing a brief notice in the local paper and setting a time to meet at a local restaurant. It doesn't take much more effort than that, and you may make some valuable contacts who could help you to grow your business faster than would be possible if you didn't network.

In addition, as briefly described earlier, many associations produce a regular publication for their members, publish special reports and literature that address particular concerns of business owners in the field, and hold regular meetings and conventions with informative seminars and the chance to network with other members. Many conventions also have trade show areas where you can visit exhibitors who offer their products and services—usually at special show discounts—that can also help your business to grow.

Benefits and Costs

The majority of associations—both general and industry-related—offer members health and life insurance, savings plans, credit card merchant privileges, discounted travel expenses, and many other business services at a discount.

All of this expertise comes at a price: annual memberships can be expensive, as well as meetings and new-member initiation fees, of course, but because they are business-related, they're fully tax-deductible. And most entrepreneurs report that the fees are worth it because of the benefits, networking opportunities, and new ideas they receive to help them enhance their own businesses.

Do It Yourself

If once you join, you find you're too busy to keep up with the regular meetings, set up a network of other entrepreneurs in your field for an e-mail round-robin. One person starts by posing a question or problem, then everyone in the round-robin chimes in to offer their take on the subject. You can even find an Internet mailing list on your subject and exchange ideas and provide leads to other people who share an interest in your business even though they may live thousands of miles away. Some prefer networking this way because of the lack of direct competition, and many entrepreneurs on active industry e-mail mailing lists report that other list members will frequently pass along leads and jobs to others when they are unable to take them on.

In any case, there are as many different solutions to a sticky business problem as there are people who are tackling that particular problem. Be open and direct with the people in your networking community; not only will you be able to hear some surprising and effective ideas that worked for them, but you may also be able to give them some advice. And that's when you know you're really a successful entrepreneur: when another business owner looks to you for advice. It will happen, and when it does, it's a great feeling.

SMART MONEY

Jim Hoskins, of Maximum Press, a computer-book publisher in Gulf Breeze, Florida, perhaps says it most eloquently when it comes to the importance of time and your business:

"*Nothing* is more valuable than your time," he says. "If you make a lot of money and have a successful business but have no time left over, you lose...I *could* do more than I am right now, but I don't want to work eighty hours a week."

Managing Your Time

You know the feeling: you spend the entire day running around from one task to another, answering phones and attending to every interruption—important or menial—that comes your way. When it's time to head home, you look back on your day and see that you weren't able to check anything off on your to-do list for that day.

Warning, another cliché ahead: If you don't manage time, time will manage you. And that can wreak havoc on the life of an entrepreneur in a big way: one of the most inefficient ways to work is to be yanked around by the urgency of one project or another, instead of you deciding which tasks take priority. In short, you need to show the projects exactly who's boss.

Of all the ways to manage your business, managing the way you spend your time and prioritizing which projects and tasks come first is probably the part of running a business that takes the most time to learn.

Start Slowly

When you first get your business up and running, especially if you're not used to juggling diverse projects, you'll need to take baby steps. The first step to successfully managing your time is to write it all down: every project, every job, even the smallest task. Write down how long you expect to have to devote to the task along with a deadline for it; it doesn't matter whether it's imposed by you or the customer. Tasks that lack a deadline tend to live in the nether regions of your schedule, always getting pushed aside for something with seemingly greater urgency. And if you know you'll get paid more quickly for certain projects, you might want to bump them up a few notches higher on your to-do list.

Control Your Agenda

Then when each workday begins, make a conscious effort to spend your time *acting*, as you work on tasks that you've put priority to, instead of *reacting* to the minor crises that come your way and turn your day into an unproductive mess. You may find this to be inordinately difficult. After all, if you have a number of people who come to you to help them solve their problems, it makes you feel good: competent and important. But if you add up all of these tiny interruptions that are infringing on your time, you may find that they can eat up more than half of your day.

What's the solution? Several things. First, you can delegate more of the decision-making responsibilities to the people who tend to come to you for help. This will make them feel more capable and they may even ask for more responsibility within a short time.

You can also make it clear that you are not to be interrupted under any circumstances other than a dire emergency, which you define. If you feel you're unable to do this, you may want to spend a weekday afternoon or more each week away from the business so you can catch up on the work that keeps getting pushed aside at the office. One book editor escapes to the reading room at a local college library whenever he needs to catch up on correspondence or read manuscripts.

SMART SOURCES

Here's where you can try before you buy. The Day-Timer Organizer software program allows you to place all of your tasks into the program, categorize them, and then cross them off the Task List it's created for you.

The Day-Runner program is also available online; it has different features from the Day Timer Organizer, so try both and then decide which, if either, is best for your needs.

www.daytimer.com/
technology/software/
download/soft1.html

www.dayrunner.com/
business/planner
4windows.html

Keep Track

Making a to-do list every day also helps. But what may be more effective is to take the longer view by keeping track of projects, appointments, and deadlines on a large wall calendar so that everyone in the office—your family, if you work at home—knows when to expect the crunch times when you may become inaccessible. You may want to color code the appointments to indicate the degree of urgency: use green magic marker to write down casual appointments and to mark the days when it's okay for people to interrupt you, yellow for major projects, and red when they can interrupt your work only if the building is on fire.

As for your weekly and daily to-do lists, it's totally up to you to decide whether you want to use a regular paper daybook, a time-management software package, or a portable personal digital assistant (PDA) that you can take with you and use to transfer data into your computer back at the office. Try both to see what works best for you; the handy thing about using a PDA is that you can set an alarm to remind you of important phone calls to make or meetings you need to attend.

Managing Meetings

Many people—employees and entrepreneurs alike—readily believe that the number one time waster in the workplace today is meetings. Whether it's a weekly staff meeting, an appointment with a potential client, or a progress report to a current customer, when you add up travel, time spent waiting for everyone to show up, and the often useless announcements and comments that seem to be standard at meetings everywhere, they are a big-time eater. And most people hate them because they start thinking of the big pile of work back at the office that has to get done immediately, or else the evening—or weekend—is shot.

Of course, there are certain situations in which a face-to-face meeting is essential, like when you're meeting with a new client or need to address some problems with your staff. But you can act to reduce the number of inconsequential meetings you attend in several ways.

One method is to simply beg off because of your workload. Recommend a focused phone conversation instead, and stress that you'll be able to give your undivided attention and be able to take immediate action after you hang up.

If you run a service-oriented business where your clients are paying you on a per-project or hourly basis, make it clear that if a regularly scheduled meeting lasts beyond a predetermined amount of time, you will charge for your time. This may also help your clients be more focused when they plan the meeting.

If you need to hold a meeting, make sure it has a definite start and finish time, and lay out the points that need to be addressed at the very beginning of the meeting. Keep an eye on the clock and try to push things along when they seem to be straggling.

But to date, the best solution involves technology, and if you can convince your clients and off-site contractors and staff to agree to using it, your meetings can be as effective as ever. Videocams that transmit over the Internet will allow for face-to-face meetings even with people who are located on the other side of the globe. You'll be able to see and hear each other and pick up on the body language and other nuances that phone conversations and e-mail often miss. Plus, you won't have to leave your office.

Undoubtedly, other methods and technologies will arise to help you to manage your time better and still accomplish your goals. Choose your weapons wisely and your business—and sanity—will thrive.

Growing Your Business

When you're first starting out, you may think expanding your business will be a great "headache" to have. You're learning to juggle even more tasks and responsibilities when it seems you don't have enough time to accomplish what's already on your plate. You may yearn for the early days of your business when things were hectic, but you still felt as though you had everything under control.

But you're getting ahead of yourself here. You don't want to expand your business in new directions until you have your current accounts and responsibilities under control, or else you won't be able to provide your current customers with the excellent service they expect. They'll be more likely to go to one of your competitors, who may not be spread so thin.

However, it is possible for you to underestimate the need for your business, and find you're swamped from day one from the overwhelming demand. While some entrepreneurs prefer slow, manageable growth as a way to learn the subtleties of running a business, others believe that rapid growth provides them with a real education on what being a business owner is all about. Besides, say quick-growth proponents, sudden growth can provide a real boost to the company when an entrepreneur may have been hesitant about forging ahead.

In any case, the key to business growth is first planning for it, and then managing and controlling its rate of expansion. Here are a few of the ways in which you can grow your business:

• Increase the geographic area to which you are marketing your business

• Adapt your current product or service to meet another niche market

• Add more products and/or services

• Compete on a higher playing field, pursuing business that larger companies automatically assume is theirs—and not yours—due to their size

Growth can be controlled; it's possible to put the brakes on if you want to grow your business at a more reasonable pace. Some of the ways you can do this is by limiting the number of customers you work with, either by booking them far in advance, or turning them down, telling them you just don't have the time. Then, pass the lead along to one of your networking buddies for brownie points from both sides. You can also limit growth by the prices you charge; by setting higher fees than your competition, you are excluding a certain segment of your market from patronizing your business. In some cases, however, you may actually attract *more* customers with higher prices, since to many peo-

WHAT MATTERS, WHAT DOESN'T

What Matters

• Staying confident that you're doing the best job you can given your time frame and resources.

• Taking a break. It may give your brain the rest it need to come up with a surefire solution to whatever problems are facing you.

• Don't take your existing customers for granted, even if they need your product or service.

What Doesn't

• Slavishly following the preliminary figures in your business plan.

• Reviewing a business plan developed and written by another entrepreneur in your same industry will unfavorably skew your perspective; you won't see all the nuances that influenced some of the factors within it.

ple a higher price is a sign of better quality, and depending upon the type of business you're in, exclusivity is a strong selling point.

More People

A big issue you'll face in growing your business is whether to hire employees, or if you already have help on board, whether to hire more staff or contract out the additional work. If you're used to doing everything yourself, letting go of some of the responsibility—both the big projects and the day-to-day stuff—can be excruciatingly painful. Just remember what you read earlier, describing a business as being the equivalent of raising and nurturing a baby? In time, though, subjected to a crushing workload, most entrepreneurs change their tune about delegating responsibility out of sheer necessity.

More Money

Another great "problem" that can actually turn into a big pain is what to do with the extra money generated by business growth. No matter how large a business becomes, some entrepreneurs will never change their stripes, and will continue to plow every extra penny directly back into their enterprise. Others will reward themselves with a trophy like a car or a new house, but then return to their old frugal ways.

The Taxman

Of course, you should expect that the Internal Revenue Service will want their share, which is why many entrepreneurs plow the money back into the business; if it's a bona fide business expense, that means it's a tax deduction, whether you spend the money on an addition to the building, more advertising, or a new employee. At the very least, you should put some of the money aside for those times in your business cycle when times aren't as flush—no matter how well your business is doing, the downtimes are inevitable.

What's Next for You and Your Business?

This is when things can get really exciting for an entrepreneur. The point at which an entrepreneur has started and established a successful business that is now running like a well-oiled machine, with happy customers and contented employees, is often the time when she starts thinking about her next venture. If there's one personality trait that entrepreneurs have in common, it's the desire to start new businesses. These people are known as entrepreneurial entrepreneurs: they're not completely happy unless they're actively working to start a new business. The challenge of starting a company from scratch and then launching it is one of the greatest satisfactions in life; you'll see, when you start your company and have been in business, even though you've experienced great ups and downs, there's still nothing better.

SMART DEFINITION

Succession
"The act or process of succeeding to the rights or duties of another." (*The American Heritage Dictionary*, third edition)

Nobody likes to think about it, but consider the issue of succession: If you suddenly die or are incapacitated and unable to run your business, who will do it for you? Succession actually involves two parts: First, you'll need to determine that your business is successful enough to continue without you; and second, you'll need to make your wishes known about your favored candidate.
   Consider this carefully; after all, without capable people to run it, a business is only worth what is generated when the tangible assets are liquidated.

Starting and running a business can be completely addictive. It's very easy to get so caught up in running your business—after all, you are giving a performance of sorts to your customers, and the attention and praise you receive in return can be very gratifying to the ego—that you may reach the point where you have absolutely no desire to spend your waking hours doing anything else. This reason is precisely why so many business owners spend eighty, even one hundred hours a week building their businesses, and why some don't hire employees even if they desperately need the help. This is also why so many entrepreneurs end up burned-out and discontented with their businesses at some point down the road.

Running a successful business—or an unsuccessful one, for that matter—is a lot more difficult than it appears on the surface. Both new and veteran entrepreneurs frequently underestimate the amount of work the business will require, while overestimating the money the business will generate. An entrepreneur who's caught between these two aspects is going to be caught in the middle when the two finally and inevitably collide.

On the whole, five years is frequently cited as the typical amount of time an entrepreneurial entrepreneur will spend on one business before feeling it's time to move on to something else.

You'll know it's time to pursue the next step when:

• You no longer become excited about a new development in your industry

• You worked through the holidays

• You've lost your enthusiasm for areas of your life

• You can't remember the last time you woke up feeling refreshed

Of course, many business owners who still love what they're doing may experience one or all of these symptoms at one time or another. The key to knowing when to move on is in tuning into your feelings. If you feel that your current venture no longer presents a challenge, or have a gnawing feeling that it's time to move on, it probably is.

Listen to all the signs, take care of yourself and your business, and try to spend at least some time each week thinking about something besides work.

Ready, Set, Go!

I know that you've been chomping at the bit to start working on your own business. Now that you have completed reading the *Smart Guide to Starting a Small Business,* you're ready.

Just as you will need to refer back to your business plan as you progress in planning and then operating your new venture, feel free to check back in with the *Smart Guide* when you need to try some new ideas, to refresh your memory about a tax issue, or just need some encouragement.

Starting your own business and then watching as it turns from a scrawny duckling into a beautiful swan—due to your own magic wand—will turn out to be one of the best things you'll accomplish in your life. Go make it happen!

THE BOTTOM LINE

Even though you have a long list of tasks to accomplish before you can "put it all together," the good news is that you're almost there. Let your enthusiasm carry you through the early stages of planning your business up through the first day you're open and beyond.

From networking to time management, to even considering the wonderfully giddy question of what you'll do after the business succeeds, you'll discover that each separate aspect of a business does indeed work as one. And when you can view your baby as a smoothly running machine, well, that is the best feeling that any entrepreneur can have.

Index

Books in the
Smart Guide™ Series

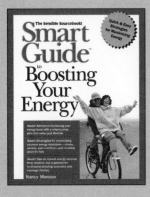
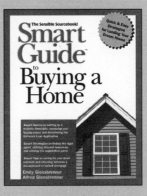

Smart Guide™ to
Boosting Your Energy

Smart Guide™ to
Buying a Home

Smart Guide™ to
Getting Strong and Fit

Smart Guide™ to
Getting Thin and
Healthy

Smart Guide™ to
Healing Foods

Smart Guide™ to
Making Wise
Investments

Smart Guide™ to
Managing Personal
Finance

Smart Guide™ to
Managing Your Time

Smart Guide™ to
Profiting from Mutual
Funds

Smart Guide™ to
Relieving Stress

Smart Guide™ to
Starting a Small Business

Smart Guide™ to
Vitamins and Healing
Supplements

Available soon:

Smart Guide™ to
Healing Back Pain

Smart Guide™ to
Maximizing Your
401(k) Plan

Smart Guide™ to
Planning for Retirement

Smart Guide™ to
Planning Your Estate

Smart Guide™ to
Sports Medicine

Smart Guide™ to
Yoga